Military Medals and Decorations

MILITARY MEDALS AND DECORATIONS

A Price Guide for Collectors

Yves Arden

RALPH CURTIS BOOKS
Hollywood, Florida, USA

**To Moira
who deserves more than one medal for
putting up with me**

First U. S. Edition by
Ralph Curtis Books
2633 Adams Street
Hollywood, Florida 33020
U.S.A.

Printed in Great Britain

CONTENTS

INTRODUCTION

There is nothing new about collecting orders, decorations and medals, and many books have been written about them during the last century. But it is only during the past ten years or so that this type of collection has become really popular. In the past, collectors were only concerned with the insignia of famous orders, which are valuable for their precious-metal content alone, or with those rarer decorations and campaign medals which have become so expensive nowadays. Decorations and medals awarded in Great Britain have always been popular with collectors, partly because they are issued direct by the King, Queen, or a high-ranking government official to the winner, and in many cases are inscribed with the name, rank and number of the recipient, and sometimes also with his regiment, ship or unit. They cannot simply be purchased from jewellers – though copies can, but these are in most cases marked. Official replacements for lost medals are also usually marked.

The policy regarding the issue of the insignia of orders, decorations and medals varies a great deal from country to country, and is very strict in many places. However, in a number of countries, it is left to the recipient of an award to purchase it himself from a jeweller, and because different firms make such insignia, inevitably there are variations in design. Belgium is a typical example. On the other hand, generally French decorations and medals are made by the French Mint. Nevertheless, one can still purchase freely from its sales office medals of campaigns of nearly a hundred years ago, but which have been struck fairly recently. Also, some manufacturing jewellers offer 'richer' models of insignia than the normal issue, so one can get a knight's breast badge of the Légion d'honneur in gold and enamel, in silver gilt and enamel, in silver and enamel, or in silver plate and enamel. This demonstrates the fact

that very different valuations can be placed on the same
item.

For these reasons, collectors must be wary: certain
gallantry awards, although seldom awarded, are not rare
when it comes to purchasing insignia manufactured freely
for collectors. The French Liberation Cross or many
German Nazi insignia of the last war are typical examples.
One can only guard against this by a careful study of the
decoration or medal, its history and, whenever possible,
by comparison with genuine contemporary examples, or
documents relating to the award.

Because of the greater interest, prices have been
rising quickly during the past few years, and collectors
are now searching for medals which only a few years ago
no one would have looked at. The market has become much
broader, and whilst the main markets remain the United
States and Great Britain, most other countries have in
their major cities at least coin shops selling medals and
often a firm specialised in this field. Whilst there has
been a great deal of literature available regarding the
subject, there has not been much said about prices. Until
fairly recently most collectors were interested in the
history attached to a medal and few looked upon it as an
investment. Now that prices have soared to record high
level, medals have become, like all other forms of
collecting, an investment which can yield better dividends
than the Stock Exchange. I sincerely hope that most
collectors will collect primarily because they are
interested in history, in research, or in brave deeds;
they should regard growth prospects as a bonus only.

Now whilst stamp or coin collectors have had the
advantage of priced catalogues for many years, this has
not been the case for medal collectors, and there has
been wide variations in price, not only from country to
country — which is to be expected — but from town to town
and dealer to dealer, many prices for the less 'classical'
items being based on the cost price. Collectors in Great
Britain have probably been more fortunate than their
fellow collectors in other countries as there has been
more information on prices published. What this book
endeavours to be is a general guide for the general
collector, so that he can have some idea of what he should

pay for most of the material he is likely to see. The
valuation brackets are based on dealers' lists, auction
prices, and prices collected recently from various
sources in the United States, Great Britain and Europe.
Unless indicated otherwise, they represent the average
price one would expect to pay for the items listed. In
particular, the following should be noted:

1 The condition of the medal

A medal in mint condition is worth more than one worn
by repeated polishing or, in the case of a decoration,
where the enamel is chipped or cracked. But one must
consider that prior to 1900 in Great Britain (the time of
the Boer War), and prior to 1914-18 in most countries,
medals were earned by regular soldiers. This is particularly the case of colonial campaigns; medals, therefore,
were more often worn on parade – and polished – than they
were later. During World Wars I and II many awards for
gallantry and medals were earned by part-time soldiers
who returned to civilian life immediately the war was over,
and who actually got their medals when they had left the
Forces and never wore them. Consequently the valuations
indicated for the earlier medals are for an average
specimen which shows signs of wear. So, for instance, a
Waterloo Medal in FDC condition would be worth more,
whilst in the case of the later medals, the valuations
are for specimens in very good condition. Those showing
sign of wear would be worth less.

2 The precious metal content and the makers

In the case of the insignia of orders, the valuations
are given, generally, for the usual finish to be expected.
But because, in many cases, the insignia of orders were
made by different firms, and also because some recipients
purchased richer types than the normal, there can be wide
variations from the prices indicated. For instance, one
can buy the star of an order normally in gold and silver
more cheaply if the insignia are only in silver and silver
gilt. Conversely the insignia of the lower grade of an
order can be worth more if it is made of richer material
than the normal issue: gold instead of silver for
instance. There are the cases too, where, as a special
mark of distinction, the insignia is set with precious

stones, or where it is made specially for a head of state,
or a member of a royal family. In the case of the
European orders, there have been well-known firms in
Austria, France, Italy, Russia etc which have produced
high standards of orders and decorations. Their name is
usually indicated on the box of issue, or on the insignia,
and can be a factor affecting the price.

3 The history attached to the medal

It is important to obtain any documents which might
be available with the medal, such as the certificate or
official document which goes with the medal, the
soldier's record of service or his military papers,
photographs, regimental histories. But documentation of
itself is not necessarily fool-proof and one must exer-
cise caution. Some regiments, or ships, distinguished
themselves in a battle and therefore the medals awarded
to those who took part will be worth more. Some regiments
too are more glamorous than others: the Marines in the
United States, the Brigade of Guards in Great Britain,
the Chasseurs Alpins in France or the Guides in Belgium,
to name but a few.

4 The identity of the recipient

When the medal is named, or when it can be
established by documentary proof, those awarded to senior
officers - or even to officers in general - to members of
the women's services, to nurses, to chaplains, to
civilians attached to a military formation, or to soldiers
with unusual ranks, are worth more than those awarded to
private soldiers or junior non-commissioned officers.

Therefore, the valuation ranges given are for
average specimens, at the bottom, and, for those which
have some of the features indicated above, at the top. But
it must be remembered that a medal which has several
special features can be worth more than indicated.
Another factor which is worth bearing in mind is that
usually a medal is worth more in its own country, for
there are likely to be more people interested in buying
it.

The problem in those countries in which there is no

established market for medals is that generally the prices
are too high. This is often the case when one buys from
antique or junk dealers who are not knowledgeable in this
field: I have often found provincial antique shops asking
more for fairly common medals than the leading specialised
dealers in London.

A growing problem in collecting medals nowadays is
the increasing number of copies and fakes which the
higher prices have brought. I purposely make a difference
between the two, because in the past, when decorations
and medals were worn more often than they are now, some
people had duplicate sets, or in some cases, if the
genuine medals had been lost, and could not be replaced
officially (for instance if lost through carelessness or
sold), others were purchased, the name erased and they
were renamed, or copies were bought from a military
tailor or a jeweller. Because of the scarcity of good
materials, these now appear on the market, and may easily
deceive collectors not too conversant with the medals in
question. In the same way, it is not uncommon to find
genuine medals with false bars — possibly amongst genuine
ones — simply because the original owner thought he was
entitled to them. These were not meant to deceive the
collector, but there are now quite a few fake medals
about which are intended to deceive and also copies of
rarer medals, originally intended only as copies, passed
off as the genuine article. This is why collectors must
beware of bargains offered in strange places and will do
better by dealing only with specialised reputable firms.
The best safeguard remains to specialise in certain
medals and to acquire as much knowledge and information
about these as possible.

The bibliography at the end of this book is a
selection only; there is a vast literature on the subject.
Good reference books are well worth having: not only can
they help safeguard one against disappointments, but they
also stimulate one's enjoyment by increasing one's
knowledge.

This book does not pretend to be a complete
catalogue; it deals only with military medals, and those
issued to both military personnel and civilians, but I
have endeavoured to cover both the United States of

America completely (as there are relatively few medals
there) and Great Britain as fully as possible, in view of
the wide interest in both these countries amongst
collectors. A few medals, such as Coronation or Jubilee
medals, are included, however, because although also
issued to civilians many were awarded to members of the
Forces and are often found in military groups of medals.
The same applies to the few police medals mentioned. Some
medals are not included because they are offered for sale
only very seldom and the majority of collectors are
unlikely to meet them. Apart from these, I have no doubt
that, in spite of my efforts, I shall have left out some
medals which should have been included; to those who spot
omissions, I offer my apologies.

Lastly, I want to acknowledge the help I have had
from Mr R. G. Aldred, who took so much trouble to produce
the eight pages of photographs which illustrate this book;
the Publications Division of the Ministry of Information
and Broadcasting of the Government of India; the Royal
Norwegian Embassy in London; the Head of the Military
Mission of the Embassy of Pakistan in London; the
Department of Defence, Canberra, Australia; and the
Military Attaché of the Portuguese Embassy in London.
All helped in providing information regarding the orders,
decorations and medals of their own country.

VALUATION CODING

Because prices vary such a great deal from one dealer to another and even more from country to country, it has been found more convenient to use a price range (or bracket), the values for which are indicated in pounds sterling and US dollars on the following table, rather than to give an exact valuation for each item. It has been explained earlier how to place individual medals within the bracket, depending on their condition or pedigree.

The date given after each medal is the date when the medal was first issued. If there is more than one date, the first date (or dates) is that of the campaign, the second, the date when the medal was issued. In some cases this can be many years after the action took place. This is an important factor in valuation because it means that such a medal is unlikely to have been worn very often on parade, therefore specimens in good condition should not be too hard to get.

In the case of orders founded many hundreds of years ago, it is obvious that there have been many changes in the insignia during these years, therefore, the price valuation, unless indicated otherwise, is for the latest type available. Early specimens will generally be more valuable, and can be accurately dated through the royal cipher found on many orders, hallmarks or designs — but this requires a special study outside the scope of this book.

CODE

£5 and under	A	₵ 9.50 and under	
From £5 to £10	B	₵ 9.50 to ₵ 19.00	
From £10 to £20	C	₵ 19.00 to ₵ 38.00	
From £20 to £30	D	₵ 38.00 to ₵ 57.00	
From £30 to £50	E	₵ 57.00 to ₵ 95.00	
From £50 to £75	F	₵ 95.00 to ₵ 142.50	
From £75 to £100	G	₵ 142.50 to ₵ 190.00	
From £100 to £250	H	₵ 190.00 to ₵ 475.00	
From £250 to £500	I	₵ 475.00 to ₵ 950.00	
From £500 to £1000	J	₵ 950.00 to ₵1900.00	
From £1000 to £2500	K	₵1900.00 to ₵4750.00	
£2500 and over	L	₵4750.00	

(Based on the rate of £1 = ₵ 1.90)

AUSTRALIA

1. <u>COLONY OF NEW SOUTH WALES MEDALS FOR BRAVERY IN
    RESISTING OR CAPTURING BUSHRANGERS</u> (1863-75)

    Obv. Victoria young head; rev.

        (a) coat of arms and legend <u>COLONY OF NEW
    SOUTH WALES</u>

        (b) small coat of arms, wreath and legend
    <u>GRANTED FOR GALLANT AND FAITHFUL SERVICES</u>.

    Named on rim or rev. Only a few medals issued.
    Ribbon: plain blue.

        Gold, rev. (a) only   J

        Silver, rev. (a) or (b) I

2. <u>MERITORIOUS SERVICE MEDALS</u>

    <u>(a) Issued by the individual Australian states
    (1894-1903)</u>

    Obv. two types: Victoria old head and Edward VII;
    rev. name of the state and the legend <u>FOR
    MERITORIOUS SERVICE</u>. Silver. Ribbon: as for the
    <u>LS&GC medals issued</u> by the states (see 3a).

        (i)   New South Wales H

        (ii) Queensland   I

       (iii) Victoria   H

        (iv) South Australia I

        (v)   Tasmania   I

<u>(b)   Issued by the Commonwealth of Australia (from
      1903)</u>

Obv. effigy of the reigning sovereign; rev. <u>FOR
MERITORIOUS SERVICE</u>. Silver. Different styles of
<u>naming, some with</u> date. Ribbon: crimson with two
central green stripes.

        (i)   Edward VII   G

        (ii)   George V   F

       (iii)   George VI   E

        (iv)   Elizabeth II D

3.   <u>LONG SERVICE AND GOOD CONDUCT MEDALS</u>

     <u>(a)   Issued by the individual Australian states
           (1894-1903)</u>

Obv. trophy of arms, Victoria young head or Edward
VII. There is very little difference in value among
the various obv; rev. name of state and legend <u>FOR
LONG SERVICE AND GOOD CONDUCT</u>. Silver. Ribbons: as
<u>indicated below</u>. Named, with date, in some cases.

        (i)   New South Wales (crimson with dark-
               blue stripe)   H

        (ii)   Queensland (crimson with light-blue
               stripe)   I

       (iii)   Victoria (plain crimson)   H

        (iv)   South Australia (plain crimson)   H

        (v)   Tasmania (crimson with pink stripe)   H

     (b)   <u>Commonwealth of Australia issue, AUSTRALIA bar
           fixed to suspender (from 1930)</u>

Rev., for all medals, <u>FOR LONG SERVICE AND GOOD</u>

CONDUCT; obv. as under. Silver. Ribbon: crimson with white edges.

    (i)   George V, military bust (1930-6)   D

   (ii)   George VI, crowned head with IND IMP in legend (1937-49)   D

 (iii)   do., but IND IMP omitted (1949-52)   D

  (iv)   Elizabeth II DEI GRA BRITT OMN in legend (1952-3)   D

   (v)   do., DEI GRATIA REGINA F D in legend (from 1953)   D

4.   EFFICIENCY MEDAL (from 1930)

Oval-shaped with bar AUSTRALIA attached to fixed suspender. Rev. FOR EFFICIENT SERVICE; obv. effigy of the reigning sovereign as below. Silver. Ribbon: green with yellow edges.

   (a)   George V, crowned bust (1930-6)   D

   (b)   George VI, crowned head with INDIAE IMP (1937-49)   D

   (c)   do., INDIAE IMP omitted (1949-52)   D

   (d)   Elizabeth II DEI GRA BRITT OMN in legend (1952-3)   D

   (e)   do., DEI GRATIA F D in legend (from 1953)   D

5.   AUSTRALIA SERVICE MEDAL 1939-45

Obv. crowned head of George VI; rev. Australian coat of arms and legend AUSTRALIA SERVICE MEDAL 1939-1945. Silver. Ribbon: dark blue, khaki and light blue, separated by two thin red stripes. Named.

6. <u>GENERAL SERVICE MEDAL</u> (1962)

With clasp <u>SOUTH VIETNAM</u> (1962-4)

  Although a British Medal it is listed here as it was only issued to Australian armed forces. This clasp was superseded by No. 7 below, authorised in 1966 to cover service after 28.5.1964

Obv. Elizabeth II crowned head, legend <u>DEI GRATIA REGINA F D</u>; rev. <u>FOR CAMPAIGN SERVICE</u>, wreath and crown. Silver. Ribbon: purple with green edges. Named   I

7. <u>AUSTRALIAN SERVICE MEDAL FOR VIETNAM</u> (1964)

Obv. as above; rev. allegorical figure and legend <u>VIETNAM</u>. Silver. Ribbon: gold with three central stripes of red and a further red stripe with blue edges. Named   D

AUSTRIA

1. <u>MILITARY ORDER OF MARIA THERESA</u> (1757)

   The senior Austrian military order which was rarely
   awarded. The insignia have the motto <u>FORTITUDINI</u>
   (for gallantry) round the Austrian colours in the
   centre. The ribbon is white with red stripes on each
   side. There were three classes, but the first two
   are seldom offered for sale, the 3rd Cl., that of
   Knight, which is a breast silver-gilt and enamel
   badge is about G.

2. <u>IMPERIAL AUSTRIAN ORDER OF THE IRON CROWN</u> (1816)

   This order originated in 1805 when it was established
   by Napoleon I, but it was revived as an Austrian
   order some ten years later by Emperor Franz I. The
   insignia consist of the Austrian double-headed eagle,
   standing on a crown with the royal cipher F in a
   shield, surmounted by crossed swords and the
   imperial crown. When awarded for military services,
   laurel wreaths are added on each side. Ribbon:
   yellow with blue edges.

   (a) Grand Cross – sash badge and breast
        star   no recent valuation

   (b) Grand Officer – neck badge and breast
        star   H

   (c) Commander – silver-gilt and enamel
        breast badge   F

   (d) Knight – silver-gilt breast badge   F

3.   <u>ORDER OF THE TEUTONIC KNIGHTS</u>

A gold and enamel black cross with white edges,
surmounted by a knight's helmet with plumes.
Suspended from a black ribbon. Awarded with swords
for military services.

      (a)   Grand Cross — sash badge and breast
           star   no recent valuation

      (b)   Grand Officer — neck badge and
           breast star   no recent valuation

      (c)   Commander — neck badge, silver and
           enamel   F

      (d)   Knight — breast badge, silver and
           enamel   D

4.   <u>BRAVERY MEDALS</u>

These were awarded in gold, in silver in two classes,
and in bronze. Although earlier types exist, details
are given below of the issue of Emperor Franz Josef I
(1848–1916) which are the ones most usually offered
for sale.

(a) 1st type (1849–59) — youthful bust of the
Emperor in uniform looking left, legend <u>FRANZ JOSEPH
I KAISER VON OSTERREICH</u> and on rev. crossed flags
with laurel wreaths and in the centre the legend
<u>DER TAPFERKEIT</u>. Ribbon: red and white with two
vertical stripes on each side and horizontal stripes
in the centre.

      (i)   gold medal, 40mm dia.   I

      (ii) silver medal, 1st Cl., 40mm dia.   E

      (iii) silver medal, 2nd Cl., 30mm dia.   C

(b) 2nd type (1859–66) — youthful bust of the
Emperor wearing whiskers and a moustache, facing left,
legend <u>FRANZ JOSEPH I V.G.G. KAISER V. OSTERREICH</u>.
Rev. and ribbon, as for 1st type.

          (iv)   gold medal   I

           (v)   silver medal, 1st Cl.   D

          (vi)   silver medal, 2nd Cl.   C

(c) 3rd type (1866-1917) - older bust of the
Emperor with whiskers and moustache, in military
uniform, facing right, with legend as 2nd type.
Rev. and ribbon as before.

         (vii)   gold medal   F

        (viii)   large silver medal   C

          (ix)   small silver medal   B

           (x)   small bronze medal   B

5.   <u>MILITARY SERVICE CROSS</u>

Long-service award. There have been several types
of this cross, which is in gilt bronze.

         (a)   for officers, 2nd Cl., for fifty years'
               service. Golden eagle superimposed on
               the centre of the cross. Smooth
               reverse   D

         (b)   do., 1st Cl., for twenty-five years'
               service. As above, but with silver
               eagle   C

         (c)   for NCOs, 2nd Cl., for sixteen years'
               service, as above but silver centre
               with fig <u>XVI</u>   C

         (d)   do., NCOs, 1st Cl., for eight years'
               service, fig <u>VIII</u> within wreath   C

6.   <u>MEDAL FOR THE CAMPAIGN AGAINST DENMARK 1864</u>

Bronze circular medal; obv. royal ciphers <u>FJ</u> (for
Franz Josef of Austria) and <u>W</u> (for Wilhelm I of
Prussia), with crowns above; rev. legend <u>UNSERN</u>
TAPFERN KRINGERN 1864 within laurel wreath. Ribbon:

black, white and orange   B

7.   <u>WAR MEDAL 1848-1916</u>

Although established in 1873, this medal was granted
for earlier campaigns and later ones, such as China
and the earlier part of WW I. Bronze circular medal.
Obv. effigy of the Emperor, with the legend <u>FRANZ
JOSEF I KAISER V OSTERREICH KONIG V. BOHMEN ETC.
APOST. KONIG. UNGARN</u>; rev. date <u>2 DECEMBER 1873</u>
within a wreath. Ribbon: black and yellow   B

8.   <u>MILITARY MEDAL OF MERIT</u> (1890)

Gilded bronze medals with a crown above; obv. effigy
of Emperor Franz Josef I, facing right, with the
legend <u>E FRANCISCUS IOS I D G IMP AUST REX BOH ET
RES APOST HUNG</u>. Rev. <u>SIGNUM LAUDIS</u> within a wreath.

     There were variations of the design of this
medal over the years. Various colour schemes of
ribbon were issued depending on the circumstances of
the award   B

9.   <u>JUBILEE COMMEMORATION MEDAL FOR THE FIFTY YEARS'
REIGN OF EMPEROR FRANZ JOSEF I</u> (1898)

Obv. effigy of the Emperor with legend as for No. 8
above; rev. <u>SIGNUM MEMORIAE</u> within a wreath and the
dates <u>MDCCCXLVIII-MDCCCXCVIII</u>.

     (a) gold, 35mm dia., surmounted by an
          eagle   I

     (b) do., in bronze, without a crown   B

10. <u>JUBILEE COURT MEDAL FOR MILITARY PERSONNEL</u> (1898)

Oval medal with the effigy of the Emperor on the
obv., without any legend; rev. <u>FRANCISCU JOSEPHUS I
QUINQVAGENARII REGNI DIEM FESTUM CELEBRANS II
DECEMBRIS MDCCCXCVIII</u>. Ribbon: red with white edges.

     (a) gold   H

(b) silver   C

(c) bronze   B

11. <u>MILITARY JUBILEE CROSS</u> (1908)

Gilt cross with on obv. the Emperor's effigy in a
medallion in the centre of the cross; rev. the dates
<u>1848-1908</u>. The cross is surrounded by a wreath.
<u>Ribbon</u>: red and white. The same cross with different
ribbons was issued to civilians   B

12. <u>COMMEMORATION CROSS</u> (1913)

Gilt bronze cross with a circular medallion in the
centre with the dates <u>1912-1913</u>; rev. plain. Ribbon:
yellow with black stripes   A

13. <u>MILITARY CROSS OF MERIT</u> (1914)

Cross with the legend <u>VERDIENST</u> on two lines in the
centre; rev. plain with the name of the maker.

     (a) 1st Cl. - silver, larger than the others.
          White and red enamel. With brooch attach-
          ment on reverse, and worn without a
          ribbon   E

     (b) 2nd Cl. - same design, but smaller and
          worn round the neck on a red and white
          ribbon   D

     (c) 3rd Cl. - bronze, breast badge, worn from
          the same ribbon   C

There are numerous variations to these medals with
additional emblems such as crossed swords, additional
small crosses, etc. These do not greatly affect the
valuation.

14. <u>IRON CROSS OF MERIT</u> (1916)

Cross made of iron awarded with or without crown.
Obv. cipher <u>FJ</u>; rev. date <u>1916</u>. Ribbon: red   B

15. <u>KARL TROOP CROSS</u> (1916)

Base-metal cross with obv. <u>GRATI — PRINCEPS ET</u>
<u>PATRIA — CAROLUS — IMP ET REX</u>; rev. legend <u>VITAM ET</u>
<u>SANGVINEM</u> and date <u>MDCCCCXVI</u>. Ribbon: red and
white   A

16. <u>BRAVERY MEDALS</u> (1917)

Obv. effigy of the Emperor Karl looking right, in
uniform; rev. legend <u>FORTUDINI</u> in a laurel wreath.

    (a) gold (real gold ones)   H

    (b) gold (but gilt bronze)   C

    (c) silver, 1st Cl.   C

    (d) silver, 2nd Cl.   B

    (e) bronze   B

Here again there are variations of these medals;
some of the silver ones are only silver-plated and
usually worth less.

17. <u>WOUND MEDAL</u> (1918)

Base-metal circular medal, with obv. effigy of
Emperor Karl and legend <u>CAROLUS</u> and rev. <u>LAESO</u>
<u>MILITI</u> with the date <u>MCMXVIII</u>. Ribbon: grey-green
with red edges   A

Only the main Austrian medals are listed which come
up for sale most frequently. There are many other
Austrian awards with many variations in ribbons,
emblems, etc, which have to be outside the scope of
this book.

BELGIUM

1. <u>ORDER OF LEOPOLD</u> (1832)

    (a) Grand Cross — eight-rays star with the arms of
    the kingdom in the centre and the motto <u>L'UNION FAIT
    LA FORCE</u> (also in Flemish in later issues) and the
    badge of the order, being the central motif of the
    star, on a Maltese cross upon an oak and laurel
    wreath, surmounted by a crown. The earlier types and
    those partly in gold are in the I bracket, later
    issues in silver G - H

    (b) Grand Officer — the badge of the order on a
    Maltese cross in silver with golden rays in between,
    the whole in the form of a breast star. Same remarks
    as above E - F

    (c) Commander — similar insignia to the badge of
    the Grand Cross, worn round the neck on a purple
    ribbon D - E

    (d) Officer — smaller version of (c) worn on a
    purple ribbon with rosette as a breast badge C

    (e) Knight — as above but silver badge and no
    rosette on the ribbon B - C The military division
    has crossed swords under the crown and above the
    Maltese cross; the naval division has crossed
    anchors; the civilian division is without either.
    Gold, silver and bronze palms can also be worn on
    the ribbon of this order, but do not affect the
    value.

2. <u>ORDER OF THE CROWN</u> (1897)

    A golden crown on blue enamel at the centre of a
    five-arm Maltese cross. Gold badge for the first

four classes, and silver for the fifth. A laurel
wreath surmounts the top arm of the Maltese cross,
except in the case of the stars. Deep-red ribbon.

    (a)   Grand Cross - star and sash badge   G

    (b)   Grand Officer - star   E

    (c)   Commander - neck badge   E

    (d)   Officer - breast badge, with rosette
          on ribbon   C

    (e)   Knight - breast badge, plain ribbon   B

Also with gold, silver and bronze palms on the
ribbon. These do not affect the value.

Below the 5th Cl. of the order there are:

    (f)   Palms in gold, silver and medals in gold,
          silver and bronze and these have the same
          ribbon, but with one broad white stripe on
          each side. These are essentially long-
          service awards, both civilian and military.
          On average   B

3.   <u>ORDER OF LEOPOLD II</u> (1900)

Very similar in design to the Order of Leopold (No.
1), except that the ribbon in the centre with the
motto <u>L'UNION FAIT LA FORCE</u> is blue instead of red
on the Order of Leopold I. The medal is overall gold-
coloured for the first four classes of the order and
silver for the fifth. The ribbon is blue with a
central black stripe.

    (a)   Grand Cross - star and badge   G

    (b)   Grand Officer - star   E

    (c)   Commander - neck badge   E

    (d)   Officer - breast badge with rosette on
          ribbon   C

(e) Knight – breast badge, ribbon without
     rosette   B

(f) There are also medals in gold, silver
     and bronze attached to this order   B

The order was originally created by Leopold II as a
house order for the then independent Congo state,
and it was only in 1909 that it became a Belgian
order. The early specimens of the insignia have the
coat of arms of the independent Congo state in the
centre and the motto TRAVAIL ET PROGRES. These are
worth about 50 per cent more than the above
valuations for the more recent insignia.

4.   ORDER OF THE AFRICAN STAR (1888)

A five-pointed star in white enamel with a blue
border, with in the centre on the obv. a five-rays
gold star on blue-enamel background; on the rev. a
red shield with the letters LL & S interwoven. Motto
TRAVAIL ET PROGRES round the gold star. The whole
upon a wreath and surmounted by a crown. Ribbon: pale
blue with a yellow stripe. Five classes:

(a) Grand Cross – breast star and badge   G

(b) Grand Officer – breast star   E

(c) Commander – neck badge   E

(d) Officer – breast badge with rosette
     on the ribbon   C

(e) Knight – silver badge, instead of gold
     for the first four classes, and ribbon
     without rosette   B

(f) There are also circular medals in gold,
     silver and bronze   B

5.   ROYAL ORDER OF THE LION (1891)

A cross pattée with white-enamel arms, edged with
metal and blue enamel, the arms separated by two Cs

interlaced. The centre has a gold crowned lion on a
blue background, surrounded by the motto of the Congo
TRAVAIL ET PROGRES. The rev. has a monogram and a
crown. The whole is surmounted by a crown and the
insignia is in gold for the first four classes and
in silver for the fifth. Ribbon: purple with narrow
stripes of pale blue, yellow and pale blue. There
are the same five classes as for No. 4 and their
valuation is in the same brackets. There are also
three equivalent medals   B

6.   IRON CROSS (CROIX DE FER) (1831-5)

The first Belgian decoration. Originally there was
an Iron Cross and an Iron Medal (octagonal), but the
latter was never made or issued, being cancelled
within eight months of its establishment and
replaced by the Iron Cross, 2nd Cl. In 1835, the 2nd
Cl. was abolished and all recipients were entitled
to the 1st Cl. cross. Ribbon: red with yellow and
black stripes on edges.

   (a)   1st Cl. Iron Cross — Maltese-type cross with
         four arms, balls at each point of the arms,
         with a shield in the centre with the Belgian
         lion, in gold, within a gold cirlce, and the
         date 1830 on the rev.   E

   (b)   2nd Cl. Iron Cross — as above but for gold read
         silver   E

Sometimes, one comes across the Order of the Star of
Honour which was established in 1831 by the
Provisional Government and abolished soon afterwards
as illegal. It was replaced by the Iron Cross, but
unofficial specimens exist and they usually have the
ribbon described above.

7.   COMMEMORATIVE CROSS FOR THE VOLUNTEERS OF 1830

Issued in 1878 to those entitled to the above cross,
who were not issued with it during the period prior
to 1835. Enamel cross similar to No. 6 above, but in
white enamel with a golden Burgundy cross in between,
the shield in black enamel, in the centre, has the

Belgian lion on the obv. and the date <u>1830</u> on the
rev. Ribbon: black with thin yellow and red vertical
stripes   D

8.   <u>MILITARY CROSS</u> (1885)

This is a long-service award for officers. A golden
cross with four arms enamelled in black, the Belgian
lion in the centre, with crossed swords and
surmounted by a crown. On the rev. the royal cipher
in the centre. The 1st Cl. has a rosette on the
ribbon, the 2nd Cl. is without rosette. The ribbon
is green with two broad red and two narrow yellow
stripes   C

9.   <u>MILITARY DECORATION</u> (1841)

Established in 1841, this decoration was modified in
1846, 1873, 1902 and 1952. Golden cross with rays
between the arms of the cross, the Belgian lion in
the centre, surmounted by a crown. There are two
classes. The 1st Cl. has an inverted <u>V</u> in gilt on
the ribbon. When awarded for distinguished service
the ribbon is scarlet, with red, yellow and black
stripes on the edges: when awarded for long service,
the ribbon is made up of narrow red, yellow and
black (Belgian national colours) stripes. Earlier
medals are worth more, but the average bracket for
either class is   B

10.   <u>CROIX DE GUERRE 1914-18</u>

Same design as No. 8, but in bronze. Ribbon: red
with five green stripes. The rev. of the cross has
the letter <u>A</u> (Albert I, King of Belgium during WW 1).
Various citations are shown by:

          a bronze lion (regimental citation)

          a silver lion (divisional citation)

          a silver gilt lion (army corps citation)

          a bronze palm (army citation)

Citation insignia make very little difference to
the value B

11. <u>CROIX DE GUERRE 1939-45</u>

Same as No. 10, but with the letter <u>L</u> on the rev.
(for Leopold III), and the ribbon is red with six
narrow green stripes. The citation emblems are
slightly different, the lion is on a small disc
instead of being cut out as in the 1914-18 cross,
and the palm has the letter <u>L</u> on it. This cross was
also awarded to the troops who took part in the
Korean War B

12. <u>CROIX DE GUERRE</u> (1954)

Similar but with a lion on the rev. instead of the
royal cipher. The ribbon is green with three red
stripes on each side   B

13. <u>YSER MEDAL</u> (1918) <u>AND YSER CROSS</u> (1934)

Issued to the troops who took part in the Yser
battles in October 1914. Obv. allegorical figure of
a warrior; rev. a lion with the word <u>YSER</u>. The medal
hangs from a medallion also with <u>YSER</u>. The medal,
which is in greenish bronze, was modified in 1934,
and four arms added to turn it into a cross. Ribbon:
red with broad black edges. For either B

14. <u>FIRE CROSS (CROIX DU FEU) 1914-18</u>

Awarded for front-line service and issued 1934. Two
oblongs crosswise. Obv. a steel helmet and bayonet;
rev. legend <u>SALUS PATRIAE SUPREMA LEX</u> with crown and
dates <u>1914-1918</u>. Bronze. Ribbon: red with three
narrow stripes of pale blue B

15. <u>MARITIME DECORATION 1914-18</u>

Cross in gold and enamel (1st Cl.) and silver and
enamel (2nd Cl.) with crossed swords behind and
letter <u>A</u> in the centre (for Albert I). Ribbon: green
with narrow red, yellow and black stripes and crossed
anchors. For either   C

30

There are also three medals in gold, silver and
bronze issued in conjunction with this decoration.
Their design is very similar to the cross and the
crossed swords are above the medal. The ribbon is
the same B

16.   VOLUNTEERS' MEDAL 1914-18

Oval-shaped bronze medal issued 1930. Obv. allegorical representation of the volunteers of 1914-18 and
of 1830; rev. legend VOLUNTARIIS 1914-1918 PATRIA
MEMOR. Ribbon: plain blue B

17.   VOLUNTEERS' MEDAL 1940-5

Circular bronze medal issued 1946. Obv. standing
soldier; rev. lion with legend VOLONTARIIS and dates
1940-1945. Ribbon: dark blue with eight red
stripes B

18.   VICTORY MEDAL 1914-1918

Obv. Winged Victory; rev. coat of arms of Allied
nations with legend LA GRANDE GUERRE POUR LA
CIVILISATION - DE GROTE OORLOG TOT DE BESCHAVING.
Ribbon: rainbow colour A

19.   COMMEMORATIVE WAR MEDAL 1914-18

Oblong medal tapering to the suspension ring with on
the obv. the head of a soldier in a steel helmet; on
the rev. the legend MEDAILLE COMMEMORATIVE DE LA
CAMPAGNE 1914-1918 and in Flemish HERRINNERINGS
MEDAILLE VAN DE VELDTOCHT. Ribbon: yellow central
stripe with black edges and two red stripes.

     This medal can have various emblems on the
ribbon: a silver-gilt crown for volunteers; silver
and silver-gilt bars for service on the front line;
red-enamel cross for wounds; silver star for those
invalided; anchor in bronze for merchant navy and
fishermen; silver-gilt bar 1916-R-1918 for service
in Russia. These add very little to the value   B

20.   MEDAL FOR THE ARAB CAMPAIGN 1892-4

Bronze circular medal. Obv. effigy of King Leopold
II, with the legend LEOPOLD II ROI SOUVERAIN DE
L'ETAT INDEPENDANT DU CONGO; rev. the legend
CAMPAGNE ARABE DE 1892-1894, surrounded by laurel
wreath. Ribbon: yellow with six light-blue stripes
C

21.   MEDAL FOR CAMPAIGN IN AFRICA 1914-17

In silver for Europeans and in bronze for natives.
Obv. standing lion surrounded by rocks, royal crown
above the medal; obv. dates 1914-16 for the first
type and 1914-17 for the second, and names of the
main battles of the campaign. Ribbon: light blue with
yellow edging. There is a bar to this medal MAHENGE
for the 1917 German East African campaign.

        (a) silver, with or without bar   C

        (b) bronze, do.   B

22.   ESCAPEES CROSS (CROIX DES EVADES) (1944)

Bronze Maltese cross, with rays between the arms; in
the centre a shield with the Belgian lion. Plain rev.
Ribbon: green with three black stripes   B

23.   RESISTANCE MEDAL 1940-5

Bronze circular medal. Obv. allegory of Resistance;
rev. laurels with the motto RESISTERE and the dates
1940-1945. Ribbon: black with green edges and two
narrow red stripes in the centre   B

24.   PRISONERS OF WAR MEDAL 1940-5

Bronze circular medal. Obv. circle with a cross in
the centre, over which is a sword with the dates
1940-1945; rev. barbed wire and chains. The medal is
surmounted by the royal crown. Ribbon: black with
vertical narrow red and yellow stripes. Bars were
awarded   B

25. MARITIME MEDAL 1940-5

Bronze circular medal, issued 1941. Obv. Belgian lion;
rev. royal cipher. Ribbon: watered olive with thin
white stripes and crossed anchors   B

26 ABYSSINIAN CAMPAIGN MEDAL 1941

Oblong bronze medal. Obv. heads of European and
African soldiers with the dates 1940-1941; rev.
battle names SAYO, GAMBELA, ASOSA. Ribbon: pale blue
with yellow edges with thin green stripes. A bar
ABYSSINIE is worn on the ribbon   B

27. AFRICAN WAR MEDAL 1940-5

Rectangular bronze, issued 1947. Obv. head of a
European and an African soldier with the dates
1940-1945. Plain rev. The following bars have been
awarded: NIGERIE, MOYEN-ORIENT, MADAGASCAR, BIRMANIE.
Air force personnel have wings above the medal.
Ribbon: gold and light blue   B

28. MEDAL FOR OVERSEAS SERVICE (1951)

Bronze and circular with obv. royal arms within a
sixteen-point star; rev. United Nations' arms within
a wreath. Ribbon: light blue with two white stripes
and the Belgian national colours on the edges. A bar
with COREE - KOREA has been issued for the Korean
War C

29. WAR VOLUNTEER MEDAL (1952)

Circular bronze with obv. allegory of a warrior
holding a sword with V in the background; rev. lion
with legend VOLUNTARIS. Ribbon: pale blue with eight
red stripes B

30. MEDAL COMMEMORATIVE OF THE 1870-1 WAR

Circular bronze medal, issued 1911. Obv. Belgian
coat of arms with the motto L'UNION FAIT LA FORCE
and on the rev. the letter A (for Albert I) with
the dates 1870-1871. Ribbon: black, yellow, red,

yellow, red, yellow, black C

31. MEDAL COMMEMORATIVE OF THE REIGN OF KING LEOPOLD II
     (1905)

     Circular gilt-bronze medal. Obv. effigy of Leopold
     II, in an oval medallion, oak and laurel wreath.
     Rev. dates (a) 1865-1905 (b) 1865-1909, 1889-1909.
     Ribbon: red with a black central stripe and a yellow
     one on each side C

32. MEDAL COMMEMORATIVE OF THE REIGN OF KING ALBERT I
     (1962)

     Bronze medal with obv. effigy of King Albert I
     wearing a steel helmet, with the legend ALBERTUS REX:
     rev. crown and royal cipher with the dates 1909-1934.
     Ribbon: gold moiré with thin centre green stripe   C

33. MEDAL COMMEMORATIVE OF THE CENTENARY OF INDEPENDENCE
     (1930)

     Silver-plated bronze medal, octagonal-shaped. Obv.
     effigies of Kings Leopold I, Leopold II and Albert
     I; rev. laurel and oak leaves. Ribbon: white with
     the Belgian national colours on the edges   C

34. SERVICE STAR (1889)

     Issued for service in the Belgian Congo. There are
     various types of this star:

         (a) silver star 30mm dia. with a gold star on
              the obv., and the motto TRAVAIL ET
              PROGRES on the rev. (1889 type)   D

         (b) the same but 40mm dia. (1910 type)   D

         (c) gold star, central medallion in white
              enamel with letters AA entwined or a
              single letter A, 40mm dia. (1910-36
              type)   C

         (d) do., but with letters LL entwined instead
              of AA (1936). There is some doubt as to

34

whether this star was actually issued
owing to WW II   no valuation

   (e)   gold star with white central medallion
        with five-pointed gold star, and on the
        rev. the motto <u>TRAVAIL ET PROGRES</u> –
        <u>ARBEID EN VOORUITGANG</u> (1956)   C

   (f)   do., silver   B

Ribbon: plain blue with horizontal silver stripe or
gold stripe, according to length of service.

35. <u>SERVICE MEDALS FOR BELGIAN CONGO NATIVE TROOPS</u> (1892)

There are several types of this medal with the
effigies of Kings Leopold II, Albert I, Leopold III
and Baudouin, in gold, silver or bronze, some with a
crown above the medal. Obv. effigy of the reigning
sovereign; rev. the arms of the Belgian Congo with
the motto <u>LOYAUTE ET DEVOUEMENT</u>. Ribbon: plain blue
with bars with stars to indicate additional lengths
of service. Valuation usually B – C

CANADA

1. <u>ORDER OF CANADA</u> (1967)

    Obv. maple leaf with the legend <u>DESIDERANTES</u>
    <u>MELIOREM PATRIAM</u> and surmounted by <u>St Edward</u>'s crown.
    <u>Gold and enamel</u>. Rev. legend <u>CANADA</u> within a circle,
    and serial number below. Unnamed. Worn round the
    neck. Ribbon: red with a central white stripe.

    Few have been awarded so far and no valuation
    is available.

2. <u>ORDER OF CANADA – MEDAL OF COURAGE</u> (1967)

    Obv. snow flake with six points within a maple leaf
    surmounted by St Edward's crown in silver and enamel;
    rev. legend <u>COURAGE</u>. Named. Ribbon: red with a
    central white stripe. No valuation is available.

3. ORDER OF CANADA – MEDAL OF SERVICE (1967)

    Obv. as above; rev. legend <u>SERVICE</u>. Ribbon: as above
    H

4. <u>CANADA MEDAL</u> (1943)

    Obv. crowned head of George VI; rev. coat of arms
    of Canada within a wreath of maple leaves surmounted
    by a crown with legend <u>CANADA</u>. Silver. Ribbon: white
    with red border stripes.

    Although a limited number of these medals were
    struck, the medal was never awarded, and there is no
    recent valuation.

5. <u>ROYAL CANADIAN CADETS AWARD FOR BRAVERY</u> (1948)

Obv. figures of sea, army and air cadets with the
legend <u>AWARD FOR BRAVERY</u>; rev. plain, engraved with
name and unit. Silver. Ribbon: dark blue, red, light
blue, red, dark blue; hanging from silver brooch with
the legend <u>CANADA</u>.

   Only a few have been awarded and no valuation
is available.

6. <u>CANADIAN VOLUNTEER SERVICE MEDAL 1939-45</u> (Illustration No. 62)

Issued 1943. Obv. marching figures representing male
and female services with the legend <u>1939 CANADA 1945
VOLUNTARY SERVICE VOLONTAIRE</u>; rev. Canada coat of
arms. Silver. Issued unnamed. A maple leaf on a
silver bar is issued for service outside Canada.
Ribbon: blue with two stripes of red and green on
each side B

7. <u>DEFENCE MEDAL</u> (1945)

Same as for Great Britain but in silver. Issued
unnamed B

8. 1939-1945 WAR MEDAL (1946)

   (a) same as for Great Britain but in silver.
        Issued unnamed   B

   (b) however, the medals issued to the
        merchant navy were named and are much
        more difficult to find   E

   (c) also, those issued to next of kin have
        a silver memorial bar with the name
        and date of death attached to the
        ribbon   C

9. <u>CANADA KOREAN WAR MEDAL</u> (1950)

Same as for Great Britain, but in silver. Named C

10. <u>CANADIAN MEMORIAL CROSS</u> (1919)

Cross patée surmounted by a wreath, with crown on
the top arm of the cross, and maple leaves on the
other three. The royal cipher is in the centre of
the cross. Rev. plain, name, rank and regimental
number engraved. Hallmarked. Silver. No ribbon.

    (a) with GRI cipher   B

    (b) G VI R cipher   C

    (c) E II R cipher   D

11. <u>MERITORIOUS SERVICE MEDAL</u> (1902)

Obv. (a) Edward VII (b) George V in field-marshal's
uniform; rev. FOR MERITORIOUS SERVICE, two laurel
leaves and an imperial crown, with the legend CANADA
above. Silver. Named. Ribbon: crimson with central
white stripe before 1916 and crimson with narrow
central white stripe and two white edges afterwards.

    (a) G

    (b) F

12. <u>LONG SERVICE AND GOOD CONDUCT MEDAL (ARMY)</u> (1902)

Obv. (a) Victoria old head (b) Edward VII (c) George
V in field-marshal's uniform; rev. legend FOR LONG
SERVICE AND GOOD CONDUCT and CANADA above. Silver.
Named. Ribbon: crimson with white central stripe.

    (a) and (b)   F

    (c)   E

13. <u>CANADIAN MEDAL FOR LONG SERVICE AND GOOD CONDUCT
(ARMY)</u> (1930)

Obv. (a) crowned head of George V in Corontation
robes (b) crowned head of George VI (c) crowned head
of Elizabeth II with legend DEI GRATIA REGINA; rev.
FOR LONG SERVICE AND GOOD CONDUCT. Scroll suspension

with the word <u>CANADA</u>. Silver. Named. Ribbon: crimson
with white edges.

(a)   E

(b) and (c)   F

14. <u>CANADIAN EFFICIENCY DECORATION</u> (1931)

Obv. oval oak wreath in silver with gold, with the
royal cipher within and surmounted by a gold crown;
rev. plain. Named. Ribbon: green with yellow central
stripe. Clasps: bar with royal cipher and crown.

(a) GRV cipher   D

(b) GRI cipher   E

(c) G VI R cipher   E

(d) E II R cipher   F

15. <u>CANADIAN EFFICIENCY MEDAL</u> (1930)

Obv. (a) crowned head of George V in Coronation robes
(b) crowned bust of George VI in Coronation robes
(c) the same as (b) but modified legend without
<u>ET INDAE IMP</u> (d) crowned head of Elizabeth II with
legend <u>DEI GRATIA REGINA</u>; rev. <u>FOR EFFICIENT SERVICE</u>.
Silver. Named. Scroll suspension with the word
<u>CANADA</u>. Ribbon: green with yellow border stripes.

(a) D

(b) E

(c) E

(d) F

16. <u>CANADIAN FORCES DECORATION</u> (1949)

Obv. (a) George VI coinage head, silver (b) Elizabeth
II uncrowned coinage head, tombac, named; rev. crown,
maple leaf and eagle, fleur de lis and the legend

40

<u>SERVICE</u>. Clasps: bar with crown and coat of arms
for additional ten years' service. Ribbon: red, with
three narrow silver stripes.

    (a) E

    (b) C

17. <u>ROYAL CANADIAN AIR FORCE LONG SERVICE AND GOOD
CONDUCT MEDAL</u> (1944)

Obv. (a) George VI coinage head (b) Elizabeth II
uncrowned coinage head; rev. eagle in flight
surmounted by crown and legend <u>FOR LONG SERVICE AND
GOOD CONDUCT</u>. Silver. Named. Clasps issued for
additional service. Ribbon: dark blue and crimson
with narrow white edge. Both E

18. <u>AIR EFFICIENCY AWARD</u> (1945)

Obv. (a) George VI coinage head (b) Elizabeth II
uncrowned coinage head; rev. legend <u>AIR EFFICIENCY
AWARD</u>. Silver. Named. <u>CANADA</u> on medal mount. Clasp
for each additional ten years' service. Ribbon: dark
green with two narrow central stripes in pale blue
Both F

19. <u>ROYAL CANADIAN MOUNTED POLICE LONG-SERVICE MEDAL</u>
(1935)

Obv. (a) crowned bust of George V in Coronation robes
with the shortened legend <u>GEORGIUS V REX ET IND : I
IMP</u> : (b) coinage head of George VI (c) the same
but modified legend <u>GEORGIUS VI D : G : BRITT : OMN :
REX : FID : DEF :</u> (d) uncrowned coinage head of
Elizabeth II; rev. badge of the RCMP with the legend
<u>FOR LONG SERVICE AND GOOD CONDUCT</u>. Silver. Named.
Clasps: plain with bronze (twenty-five years), silver
(thirty) and gold (thirty-five) star.

All types E

(d) is seen more often

20. <u>CANADA CENTENNIAL MEDAL</u> (1967)

42   Obv. royal cipher E II R with crown and maple leaf.
Legend <u>CONFEDERATION — CANADA — CONFEDERATION</u>; rev.
coat of arms of Canada above dates <u>1867-1967</u>. Silver.
Unnamed. Ribbon: white and red vertical stripes   D

CZECHOSLOVAKIA

1. <u>ORDER OF THE WHITE LION</u>

    Awarded to foreigners only.

    (a) 1st Cl. - a chain, normally awarded to
         heads of state   no recent valuation

    (b) 2nd Cl. - Grand Cross, a star with a
         silver lion in the centre on a coloured-
         enamel background with the legend
         <u>PRAVDA VITEZI</u>   H

    (c) 3rd Cl. - worn round the neck. A star with
         five rays terminating in small globes
         with a silver lion in the centre. The
         rays are of red enamel and split in
         three, each ray with the name of a
         province   E

    (d) 4th Cl. - similar but breast badge with
         a rosette on the ribbon   D

    (e) 5th Cl. - breast badge without
         rosette   D

    The badge is surmounted by crossed swords when
    awarded for military achievement.

2. <u>REVOLUTIONARY CROSS</u> (1918)

    Bronze cross with the angel of peace standing on a
    serpent on the obv.; man on a horse holding a flag
    on the rev. The following bars were awarded: <u>L.E.</u>,
    <u>ALSACE</u>, <u>ARGONNE</u>, <u>BACHMATCH</u>, <u>DOSS ALTO</u>, <u>SIBERIE</u>,
    <u>ZBOROV</u>. Ribbon: red, with a central white stripe
    edged in blue C

3.   <u>WAR CROSS</u> (1918)

Made up of four interwoven rings, each with the coat
of arms of the provinces. Ribbon: red and white
vertical stripes B

4.   <u>WAR CROSS</u> (1939)

Bronze cross with a lion on a shield in the centre
and crossed swords on the obv., and the Bohemian
lion and date <u>1939</u> on the rev., with the shields of
the provinces on each arm. Ribbon: thin red, white
and blue vertical stripes B

5.   <u>MEDAL FOR VALOUR</u> (1940)

Circular bronze medal with obv. lion's head, upright
sword and legend <u>ZA CHRABROST</u>; rev. legend <u>PRAVDA
VITEZI</u> and the date <u>1939</u> B

6.   <u>MILITARY MEDAL OF MERIT</u>

Awarded in silver or in bronze with obv. three heads
wearing helmets with the legend <u>ZA ZASLUHY</u> and the
initials <u>C.S.R.</u> below. Ribbon: blue with two white
stripes <u>B</u>

7.   <u>COMMEMORATIVE MEDAL OF THE 1939-45 WAR</u>

Bronze medal with a sword within a wreath and the
Czech lion. Ribbon: red with black edges B

8.   <u>VICTORY MEDAL 1914-1919</u>

Bronze medal gilt, with the usual winged-victory
pattern. Ribbon: rainbow type similar to all the
other WWI victory medals B

9.   <u>COMMEMORATIVE MEDAL FOR THE VOLUNTEERS OF WW I
1918-19</u>

Plain bronze cross with the Czech lion on a shield
in the centre. Ribbon: pale blue with red and white
edging B

DENMARK

1. <u>ORDER OF THE ELEPHANT</u> (1464)

The most senior Danish order, which in its present
form dates back to 1693. The badge consists of an
elephant in gold, enamelled white, with blue harness
and carpet, and a gold tower above. A small native
figure dressed in purple and holding a spear sits on
it. The cipher of the reigning king is on the rev.
of the figure. There is a cross in diamonds on the
obv. The star has eight points and is in silver. It
has a small silver cross surrounded by a wreath on
a red enamel background. The collar consists of
alternate elephants and towers. The sash of the order
is plain light blue.

The order is only awarded on rare occasions and
is returnable when the holder dies. Sometimes,
privately made copies are offered for sale, but there
is no recent valuation – in any case much would
depend on the metal it is made of, the maker, the
workmanship and the period.

2. <u>ORDER OF DANNEBROG</u> (1671)

There have been many changes in the statutes of the
order: January 1808, June 1808, 1812, 1842, 1861,
1912, 1951, 1952, 1964. These have modified the
insignia and the conditions of award. The cipher of
the reigning king appears on the insignia of this
order, and it can thus be dated as follows:

Frederick VI (F VI) – 1808–39

Christian VIII (C VIII) – 1839–48

Frederick VII (F VII) – 1848–63

Christian IX (C IX) – 1863–1906

Frederick VIII (F VIII) — 1906–12

Christian X (C X) — 1912–47

Frederick IX (F IX) — 1947–71

Margarethe (M) — 1971

Over the years, the many changes in the insignia
make it impossible to give a detailed valuation here,
especially as the order should be returned on the
death of the recipient, and therefore is not often
offered for sale. The following are purely an
indication:

(a) Grand Cross — sash badge in gold and
     enamel, silver breast star with enamelled
     cross superimposed, complete with full-
     dress sash. Post–1906 period   J

(b) Embroidered Star — in silver (pre–
     1909)   I

(c) Silver Cross — without enamel   E

Ribbon: white with red edges.

3.   <u>MEDAL OF MERIT</u> (1845)

A very rare medal awarded in gold or silver, bearing
the effigy of the sovereign on the obv., and the
legend <u>FORTIENT</u> within a wreath on the rev. It is
rarer still with a crown above the medal. Ribbon:
red with a vertical centre white stripe and another
horizontal. Amongst these the most common are
Christian IX (1912–47) in silver and Frederick IX
(1947–71) in silver, but even these are very seldom
offered for sale and their value is estimated at I.
This medal exists with bar, mainly in connection with
Greenland exploration and in most cases only a few
bars were awarded. Medals with bars have been issued
since 1906. Probably in the K–L brackets, with bars;
I–J without.

4.   <u>MEDAL FOR HEROIC DEEDS</u> (1793)

Issued for wearing since 1845. Awarded in gold or
silver. Same ribbon. Again this is a very rare medal.

46

Obv. the effigy of the reigning sovereign; rev. the
legend FOR AEDEL DAAD. As so few have been awarded,
they are very seldom offered for sale, and one can
only guess at a valuation in the brackets K-L,
according to the metal and/or the period.

5. MEDAL OF MERIT FOR THE BATTLE OF COPENHAGEN 1801

Obv. coat of arms, legend MODET VAERGER den 2den
April 1801; rev. crown, sword and sceptre and legend
KONGEN HAEDRER – FAEDRELANDET – SKIÖNNER. Ribbon: as
for No. 3.

       This medal is very rare and was awarded in gold
with brilliants (one only), in gold and in silver.
Some were issued without ring, and were not intended
to be worn   K

6. MEDAL FOR THE WAR OF 1848–50 (Illustration No. 1)

Bronze circular medal, issued 1877. Obv. effigy of
Frederick VII; rev. legend FOR DELTAGELSE I KRIGEN
1848–50. Ribbon: one broad and two narrow vertical
white ones   C

7. MEDAL FOR THE WAR OF 1864 (Illustration No. 2)

Bronze circular medal, issued 1877. Obv. effigy of
Christian IX; rev. legend FOR DELTAGELSE I KRIGEN
1864. Ribbon: as above   C

8. COMMEMORATIVE MEDAL FOR THE WARS 1848–50 AND 1864

Bronze circular medal, issued 1877. Obv. conjointed
busts of Christian IX and Frederick VII; rev. FOR
DELTAGELSE I KRIGEN 1848–1850 – 1864. Ribbon: as
above   E

9. KING CHRISTIAN X'S MEDAL FOR PARTICIPATION IN THE
    WAR 1940–5

Silver circular medal surmounted by a crown. Obv.
effigy of Christian X with the legend CHRISTIAN X
MIN GUD MIT LAND MIN AERE; rev. legend FOR DELTAGELSE

i ALLIERET KRIGSTJENESTE 1940-5. Ribbon: two broad
and three narrow red vertical stripes on a white
background E

10. MEDAL FOR GOOD SERVICE IN THE NAVY (1801)

Three types; all in silver. Same ribbon. Stripes: one
red, one white, one red.

    (a) 1801-14 Obv. 29 IAN 1801 CR VIII
         FOR GOD TIENESTE Rev. 25 AAR
    (b) 1814-43 Same obv. but TJENESTE for
         TIENESTE
    (c) since 1843
         As above, but 29 JAN 1801 instead of
         29 IAN 1801

These medals are returnable on the death of the
recipient, and therefore seldom offered for sale H

11. MEDAL FOR GOOD SERVICE IN THE ARMY (1945)

Silver medal similar to No. 10, but the obv. reads
26 SEPTEMBER 1870 - CR X - FOR GOD TJENESTE. Same
ribbon. Also returnable G

12. MEDAL FOR GOOD SERVICE IN THE DEFENCE (1953)

Silver, similar to No. 10, but obv. reads 11 MARTS
1953 - FR IX - FOR GOD TJENESTE. Same ribbon. Also
returnable G

13. MEDAL FOR GOOD SERVICE IN THE AIR FORCE (1953)

Same as No. 12 G

14. HOMEGUARD GOOD SERVICE MEDAL (1959)

Obv. crowned FR IX; rev. homeguard badge surmounted
by a crown with legend FORTJENT. Silver with ribbon
of two broad red stripes on the edges and narrow red
and white ones in between F

48

1 obv. DENMARK, Medal for the War of 1848–50, bronze

2 rev. DENMARK, Medal for the War of 1864, bronze

3 obv. FINLAND, Medal of Liberty, 2nd Cl., bronze

4 obv. ITALY, Messina Earthquake Medal, silver

5 obv. ITALY, Victory Medal 1915–18, bronze

6 obv. GERMANY, South West Africa Campaign Medal 1904–6, with bar 'KALAHARI 1908', bronze gilt

7 obv. GERMANY, War Merit Cross, in bronze with crossed swords

8 obv. GERMANY, do., without swords

9 obv. GERMANY, War Merit Medal, bronze

10 obv. FRANCE, Médaille de Haute-Silésie 1921, bronze

11   obv. FRANCE, Légion d'honneur, Chevalier's badge,
     Napoléon III issue, silver, enamel, with gold centre

12   obv. FRANCE, Médaille militaire, 3rd Republic's issue,
     silver and enamel

13   obv. FRANCE, Croix de Guerre 1914–18, with bronze star
     for regimental citation, bronze

14   obv. FRANCE, St Helena Medal, bronze

15   obv. FRANCE, Medal for the Mexico Expedition 1862–3,
     silver

16   obv. FRANCE, Medal for the Italian Campaign of 1859,
     silver

17   obv. FRANCE, Medal for Tonkin Campaign 1883–93,
     silver

18   rev. FRANCE, Medal for the Dahomey Campaign 1892,
     silver (note the fixing pin found on many French medals)

19   obv. FRANCE, Medal for the China Campaign of 1900–1,
     silver

20   obv. FRANCE, Colonial Medal with four bars, silver

15. <u>DISTINGUISHED FLYING MEDAL</u> (1962)

Obv. crown and royal cipher <u>FR IX</u> with legend
<u>FOR UDMAERKET LUFTTJENESTE</u>; rev. legend <u>FORTJENT</u>.
Circular silver medal. Ribbon: diagonal white and
red stripes.

    Very few of these have been awarded; they are
returnable on death of the recipient and none has
been offered for sale.

16. <u>FAITHFUL SERVICE DECORATIONS FOR NCOs</u> (1817)

  (a) eight years' medal, 1st type – brass,
       black lacquered. Obv. royal cipher <u>FR VI</u>
       with crown; rev. legend <u>FOR 8 AARS TROE</u>
       <u>TIENESTE</u>

  (b) eight years' medal, 2nd type – as above
       modified coat of arms

  (c) eight years' medal, 3rd type – as above,
       but royal cipher <u>CR VIII</u> on obv.

These medals have no ribbon, but are suspended from
chains. Many of them are in polished brass, and there
are small variations in pattern F

17. <u>FAITHFUL SERVICE DECORATIONS FOR NCOs</u> (1817)

  (a) sixteen years' cross, 1st type – brass
       cross, black lacquered. Obv. <u>FOR 16 AARS</u>
       <u>TROE – TIENESTE</u> with royal cipher <u>FR VI</u>
       in centre; rev. plain except for date <u>1817</u>

  (b) sixteen years' cross, 2nd type – as above
       with royal cipher <u>CR VIII</u>.

Also suspended from chains. There are also variations
in pattern of these crosses F

    There are also some faithful service clasps for
NCOs instituted in 1842 for twelve and twenty years'
service, but these are not medals in the true sense.
All these (Nos. 16, 17 and clasps) are returnable on
the death of the recipient.

18. <u>FAITHFUL SERVICE DECORATIONS FOR NCOs</u> (1848)

From that date a cross was awarded for both eight
and sixteen years' service, the difference being
that the eight years' has an 8 in the centre, the
sixteen years' has rays between the arms of the cross
and 16 in the centre. These are suspended from a
ribbon identical to No. 5. Rev. is plain.

      (a) <u>F VII</u> eight years' cross

      (b) <u>F VII</u> sixteen years' cross

      (c) <u>C IX</u> eight years' cross

      (d) <u>C IX</u> sixteen years' cross

      (e) <u>F VIII</u> eight years' cross

      (f) <u>F VIII</u> sixteen years' cross

      (g) <u>C X</u> eight years' cross

      (h) <u>C X</u> sixteen years' cross

      (i) <u>F IX</u> eight years' cross

      (j) <u>F IX</u> sixteen years' cross

There are variations of these medals, which are also
returnable at the death of the recipient D

19. <u>KING CHRISTIAN IX MEMORIAL BADGE</u> (1907)

Silver badge with royal cipher <u>C IX</u> in gilt. Plain
reverse. Worn without ribbon as the star of an
order. Very few were awarded J

20. <u>KING CHRISTIAN IX MEMORIAL MEDAL</u> (1906)

Silver circular medal. Obv. effigy of the King with
legend <u>CHRISTIAN IX KONGE AF DANMARK</u>; rev. <u>MED GUD
FOR AERE OG RET – 8 APRIL 1818 – (cross) – 29 JANUAR
1906</u>. Ribbon: narrow white stripe of red background
H

21. <u>KING FREDERICK VIII MEMORIAL BADGE</u> (1912)

Similar to No. 19, but with cipher <u>F 8</u>   J

22. <u>KING FREDERICK VIII MEMORIAL MEDAL</u> (1912)

Silver circular medal. Obv. <u>FREDERICUS VIII – REX
DANIAE</u>; rev. <u>3 JUNI 1843 – (cross) – 14 MAJ 1912</u>.
Ribbon: as No. 3 H

23. <u>KING CHRISTIAN X MEMORIAL BADGE</u> (1947)

Similar to No. 19 but with cipher <u>C X</u> J

24. <u>KING CHRISTIAN X MEMORIAL MEDAL</u> (1947)

Silver circular medal. Obv. <u>CHRISTIANUS X – REX
DANIAE</u>; rev. 20 APRIL 1947. <u>Ribbon</u>: as No. 3 H

25. <u>KING CHRISTIAN IX CENTENARY MEDAL</u> (1918)

Obv. King's effigy with legend <u>CHRISTIANUS IX – REX
DANIAE</u>; rev. <u>MED GUD – FOR – AERE OG RET</u>. Ribbon: as
for No. 3, with bar <u>1818 – 8 APRIL – 1918</u> G

26. <u>SLESVIG MEDAL</u> (1920)

Silver circular medal. Obv. King's effigy with
legend <u>CHRISTIANUS X – REX DANIAE</u>; rev. <u>SLESVIG 1920</u>.
Ribbon: red, white, red vertical stripes D

27. <u>KING FREDERICK VIII CENTENARY MEDAL</u> (1943)

Silver circular medal surmounted by a crown. Obv.
King's effigy with legend <u>FRIDERICUS VIII REX DANIA</u>;
rev. <u>DOMINUS – MIHI – ADLUTOR</u>. Ribbon: as No. 3 with
bar <u>1843 – 3 JUNI – 1943</u> G

28. <u>KING CHRISTIAN X MEDAL IN COMMEMORATION OF THE
LIBERATION</u> (1946)

Silver circular medal surmounted by a crown. Obv.
King's effigy with legend <u>CHRISTIANUS X – REX DANIAE</u>;
rev. <u>PRO DANIA – 1940–45</u>. Ribbon: as for No. 26 C

29. <u>GALATHEA MEDAL</u> (1954)

Silver circular medal. Obv. King's effigy and legend
<u>FRIDERICUS IX REX DANIAE</u>; rev. <u>GALATHEA 1950–1952</u>.

Ribbon: as No. 3   E

30. <u>KOREA MEDAL</u> (1956)

Silver circular medal with obv. as above; rev.
<u>JUTLANDIA – KOREA 1951–1953</u> and wreath. Ribbon: red
with two white vertical stripes   E

FINLAND

1. <u>ORDER OF THE CROSS OF LIBERTY</u>

   No longer issued.

   (a) Grand Cross of the Order of the Cross of
       Liberty - sash badge and star
                                    no recent valuation

   (b) Mannerheim Cross, 1st Cl., of the Order
       of Liberty   no recent valuation

   (c) Cross of Liberty, 1st Cl., with star D

   (d) Mannerheim Cross, 2nd Cl., of the Order
       of Liberty   no recent valuation

   (e) Cross of Liberty, 1st Cl.   D

   (f) Medal of Liberty, 1st Cl., with
       rosette   D

   (g) Medal of Merit in gold of the Cross of
       Liberty   F

   (h) Cross of Liberty, 2nd Cl.   C

   (i) Cross of Liberty, 3rd Cl.   C

   (j) Cross of Liberty, 4th Cl., for war-time
       merit   C

   (k) Medal of Liberty, 1st Cl.   C

   (l) Medal of Liberty, 2nd Cl. (Illustration
       No. 3)   B

2. <u>ORDER OF THE WHITE ROSE</u> (1919)

   Rose in the centre of a white enamel cross with lions
   in gold between the arms. Ribbon: blue.

(a) Grand Cross, with Collar of the White
     Rose of Finland. Rare no recent valuation

(b) Grand Cross of the White Rose of Finland,
     breast star and sash badge   H

(c) Commander, 1st Cl., of the White Rose of
     Finland, neck badge and breast star   F

(d) Commander, neck badge only   E

(e) Knight, 1st Cl.   D

(f) Cross of Merit   C

(g) Knight   C

(h) Medal, 1st Cl., in gold with clasp   E

(i) Medal, 1st Cl., with clasp   B

(j) Medal, 2nd Cl., with clasp   B

These last three medals are also without clasps,
same valuation.

3. <u>MEDAL FOR THE CAMPAIGN AGAINST SOVIET RUSSIA</u>
    (1918)   B

4. <u>WAR MEDAL 1939-40</u>

In bronze, legend <u>KUNNIA ISANMAA</u>   B

5. <u>WAR MEDAL 1941-5</u>

Obv. a bayonet with leaf; rev. legend <u>ISANMAA</u>
<u>1941-45</u>   B

FRANCE

1.   <u>LEGION D'HONNEUR</u> (1804)

There are many minor variations of the insignia of
this order, the main types being the following:

(a)   1804-6 - Napoléon I large head within a
circle with the legend <u>NAPOLEON EMP DES</u>
<u>FRANCAIS</u> on the obv., and an Imperial
eagle on the rev. at the centre of a white
enamelled five-pointed cross with laurel
wreath behind. The cross suspended by a
ring to the ribbon. Eagle faces left   I

(b)   1806 - smaller head of Napoléon I in the
centre, and the star is surmounted by
the imperial crown which is attached
to it   H

(c)   1808 - different design of crown,
surmounted by a cross, and with fleur de
lis at the base of each arch of the crown.
The eagle faces right   H

(d)   1811 - larger badge with small balls at
the end of each point of the star   H

(e)   1814 - same as the 1808 type, but with
the effigy of Henry IV on the obv.
instead of Napoléon I and the legend
<u>HENRI IV ROI DE FRANCE ET DE NAVARRE.</u>
On the rev. three fleurs de lis instead
of the eagle   F

(f)   1816-30 - as above but with balls at the
end of the points of the cross - as for
type (d). The cross at the top of the
crown is changed for a fleur de lis, and
fleurs de lis appear at the bottom of the
arches of the crown   E

(g) 1830-48 - obv. legend becomes <u>HENRI IV</u>,
     and the rev. has crossed tricolor flags
     instead of the fleurs de lis. There is no
     longer a fleur de lis on the top of the
     crown   E

(h) 1848-51 - small head of Napoleon I with
     legend <u>BONAPARTE PREMIER CONSUL 19 MAI 1802.</u>
     On the rev. the legend <u>REPUBLIQUE FRANCAISE</u>
     and <u>HONNEUR ET PATRIE</u> below the crossed
     flags in the centre disc   F

(i) 1851-2 - ob. unchanged but on the rev. the
     imperial eagle appears again with the
     original legend, its head to the left.
     Crown with fleurs de lis   F

(j) 1852-70 - eagles at the base of the crown;
     obv. legend <u>NAPOLEON EMPEREUR DES FRANCAIS.</u>
     Eagle's head to the right (Illustration
     No. 11)   F

(k) 1870 - an enamel oak wreath replaces the
     crown above the star, and Ceres now
     appears in the centre of the obv. with the
     legend <u>REPUBLIQUE FRANCAISE 1870.</u> Crossed
     tricolor flags on the rev.   C

(l) 1951 - the date 1870 is removed from obv.
     legend   C

(m) 1962 - the date <u>29 FLOREAL AN X</u> appears
     instead   C

The above valuations are for the straightforward
issue of the 5th Cl, the Chevalier's grade, which is
enamel on silver. One can find richer-type insignia,
some in gold, which is more valuable. It must be
remembered that there are numerous variations of the
insignia of this order.

Originally there were two classes, the silver
star or small eagle, and the star or gold eagle. In
1805 a third one was added the Grande Décoration or
Great Eagle. Since 1816, there have been five classes:

     (i) Grand Croix (1st Cl.) - gold badge and
          sash   I
          breast silver star   G

(ii) Grand Officer (2nd Cl.) - gold badge
      and sash   H
      breast silver star   G

(These valuations are for insignia type (k) onwards)

(iii) Commander (3rd Cl.) - neck badge,
      type (j)   H
      type (k) and later   E

(iv) Officer (4th Cl.) - breast badge with
      rosette, type (j)   F
      type (k) and later   D

(v)   Chevalier (Knight) (5th Cl.) - breast
      badge without rosette. Valuation as
      indicated under types (a) to (m)

Ribbon: plain red, moiré.

2. ORDER OF THE LIBERATION (1940)

One class only that of Companion. The insignia called
'The Liberation Cross', with bronze sword with the
Lorraine cross superimposed, over a plain bronze
square. Rev. the legend PATRIAM SERVANDO VICTORIAN
TULIT.

        The order has not been awarded since 1946, and
altogether 1,053 crosses were awarded. The insignia
are not rare as they can be purchased from the
French Mint   C

3. MEDAILLE MILITAIRE (1852)

The equivalent of a distinguished conduct medal,
awarded only to general officers or admirals
commanding a fleet, and to NCOs who distinguished
themselves in time of war. It is a silver medal, of
which there are three types:

(a)   Second Empire, Napoléon III (1852-70) -
      effigy of Napoléon III in the centre
      surrounded by wreath, the medal being
      surmounted by the imperial eagle looking
      right   D

(b) Third Republic (1870-1951) (Illustration
     No. 12) - effigy of Ceres with the legend
     REPUBLIQUE FRANCAISE - 1870. The eagle
     above the medal is replaced by a trophy of
     arms, which generally swivels, but some
     types are fixed   C

(c) Fifth Republic (from 1951) - as above,
     but without the date 1870   C

Ribbon: yellow with green edges.

4. CROIX DE GUERRE (1915) (Illustration No. 13)

    (a) World War I type - bronze cross with
         crossed swords between the arms of the
         cross, in the centre the head of Ceres with
         the legend REPUBLIQUE FRANCAISE, on the
         rev. dates 1914-15, 1914-16, 1914-17 or
         1914-18. Ribbon: green with thin red
         stripes. This medal was awarded for
         mentions in despatches, and the type of
         despatch is indicated by an emblem on the
         ribbon: bronze star for regimental despatch,
         silver star for divisional despatch,
         silver gilt for army corps despatch, small
         bronze laurel branch for army despatch.
         Five bronze palms are exchanged for a
         silver one. Several emblems can be worn on
         the same ribbon. The dates or the emblems
         do not affect the value   B

    (b) World War II type, Vichy issue (1939-40) -
         same type but with the dates 1939-40 on
         the rev.   B

    (c) World War II type, Free French issue - do.,
         no date on rev   B

    (d) World War II, 1939-45, definitive issue -
         ribbon: red with four green stripes   B

All these have the same types of emblems for
citations as the WW I issue.

5.   CROIX DE GUERRE DES THEATRES D'OPERATIONS EXTERIEURES
      (1921)

      The same medal, but for overseas service. The obv.
      is the same, but the rev. has the legend THEATRE
      D'OPERATIONS EXTERIEURES instead of the dates, and
      the ribbon is red with a broad blue central stripe.
      Same emblems on the ribbon   B

6.   ST HELENA MEDAL (1857) (Illustration No. 14)

      Awarded in 1857 to the soldiers who had taken part
      in the wars from 1792 to 1815. It is in bronze with
      Napoléon I's head, and has legend on rev. CAMPAGNES
      DE 1792-1815 A SES COMPAGNONS DE GLOIRE, SA DERNIERE
      PENSEE, SAINT HELENE 5 MAI 1821. The ribbon is the
      same as that of the Croix de Guerre, WW I. There are
      various types of this medal, some in bronze gilt,
      but generally value is   C

7.   MEDAILLE D'ITALIE (1859) (Illustration No. 16)

      Silver circular medal, obv. effigy of Napoleon III;
      rev. names of the main battles: MONTEBELLO, PALESTRO,
      TURBIGO, MAGENTA, MARIGNAN, SOLFERINO and the legend
      CAMPAGNE D'ITALIE 1859   C

8.   MEDAILLE DE CHINE (1860)

      Silver circular medal of the same type as above, but
      with the legend EXPEDITION DE CHINE 1860 and names
      of the battles TA-KOU, CHANG-KIA-WAN, PA-LI-KAO,
      PE-KING on rev.

          The ribbon is unusual as it has the two Chinese
      characters, Pe Kin, in blue on a background of yellow.
      To my knowledge only a few original ribbons exist,
      so the medal is more valuable complete with
      ribbon   C

9.   MEDAILLE DU MEXIQUE (1863) (Illustration No. 15)

      Similar to the above two. On rev. legend EXPEDITION
      DU MEXIQUE 1862-3, and the names of the battles

CUMBRES, CERRO-BORREGO, SAN LORENZO, PUEBLA, MEXICO.
White ribbon with the Mexican eagle in black holding
a green snake in its beak. Same remarks regarding
the ribbon as for No. 8   C

10.   TONKIN MEDAL 1883-93 (1895) (Illustration No. 17)

       Circular silver medal with obv. female effigy of
       the republic with the legend REPUBLIQUE FRANCAISE;
       on the rev. the legend TONKIN CHINE ANNAM 1883-1885
       and the names of the battles SONTAY, BAC-NINH,
       FOU-TCHEOU, FORMOSE, TUYEN-QUAN, PESCADORES. The
       naval issue of this medal has additionally the name
       CAU GIAI. Same valuation. Ribbon: yellow and green
       vertical stripes   C

11.   MADAGASCAR MEDAL (1885-95)

       Similar circular silver medal to the above.

            (a)   1st campaign with MADAGASCAR 1885-6
                  on rev.   C

            (b)   2nd campaign, do., but with ornate bar
                  1895   C

       Ribbon: horizontal light-blue and green stripes.

12.   DAHOMEY MEDAL (1892) (Illustration No. 18)

       Similar to the previous two medals, in silver, with
       on rev. the name DAHOMEY. Ribbon: vertical black and
       yellow stripes   C

13.   COLONIAL MEDAL (1893) (Illustration No. 20)

       General service medal issued from 1893 onwards to
       cover small wars or expeditions in Asia and Africa.
       Always issued with a bar, up to 1914; after can be
       issued without. Obv. republic's head with the legend
       REPUBLIQUE FRANCAISE and on the rev. a trophy with
       a terrestial globe, and the legend MEDAILLE COLONIALE.
       The suspension is generally in the form of laurel
       branches, but it also exists with a plain ring. The
       diameter of the medal varies, and some specimens are
       stamped ARGENT (silver).

60

(a) gold bar DE L'ATLANTIQUE A LA MER
     ROUGE   E

(b) silver-gilt bars MAROC 1925, MAROC
     1925-1926 either   D

(c) silver bars: MAROC, ADRAD, CENTRE AFRICAIN,
     AFRIQUE EQUATORIALE FRANCAISE, AFRIQUE
     OCCIDENTALE FRANCAISE, ALGERIE, COMORES,
     GABON-CONGO, CONGO, COTE DES SOMALIS, COTE
     D'IVOIRE, COTE DE L'OR, DAHOMEY, GUINEE
     FRANCAISE, GUYANE, LAOS ET MEKONG, TONKIN,
     COCHINCHINE, INDOCHINE, EXTREME-ORIENT,
     MADAGASCAR, ILES MARQUISES, MAURITANIE,
     SENEGAL ET SOUDAN, NOSSI-BE, NOUVELLE-
     CALEDONIE, ILES DE LA SOCIETE, TCHAD,
     TUNISIE, SOMALIE, LYBIE, ERYTHREE, KOUFRA,
     FEZZAN, ETHIOPIE, BIR-HAKEIM 1942, FEZZAN-
     TRIPOLITAINE, TUNISIE 1942-43, AFRIQUE
     FRANCAISE LIBRE.

Some of the original bars are quite scarce, but as
these medals and bars can still be purchased from
the Paris Mint, the average value of this medal with
up to six bars is   C

Ribbon: blue with white stripes.

     In 1962, this medal became the MEDAILLE D'OUTRE-
MER, with the same design and ribbon, but the new
legend instead of MEDAILLE COLONIALE.

14. MOROCCO MEDAL (1909)

Silver circular with an obv. slightly different from
the previous one, and the rev. has the legend MAROC
with a military design. The following silver bars
have been issued CASABLANCA, OUDJA, HAUT-GUIR, MAROC.
Ribbon: green with white stripes   C

15. MEDAL FOR THE 1870-1 WAR (1911)

Circular bronze medal; obv. effigy of the republic;
rev. military and naval trophy with the dates

1870-1871. Volunteers are entitled to the silver bar
ENGAGES VOLONTAIRES. Ribbon: alternate green and
and black vertical stripes   B

16. GENEVA CROSS 1870-1

Issued by the French Society for Succouring the
Wounded and not by the French government, but
recognised all the same. Issued in silver and in
bronze. Obv. dates 1870 and 1871 and the legend
SOCIETE FRANCAISE DE SECOURS AUX BLESSES DES ARMEES
DE TERRE ET DE MER; rev. plain, sometimes named.
The ribbon is white with a red cross in the centre C

17. COMMEMORATIVE MEDAL OF THE GREAT WAR 1914-18 (1920)

Bronze medal with obv. female figure wearing a
helmet and holding a sword; rev. legend GRANDE GUERRE
1914-1918 and REPUBLIQUE FRANCAISE. Volunteers
received a white metal bar ENGAGE VOLONTAIRE. Ribbon:
red and white vertical stripes   B

18. MEDAILLE DU LEVANT 1918-21 (1922)

Also called MEDAILLE COMMEMORATIVE DE SYRIE-CILICIE.
Obv. and rev. are the same as for No. 14, but with
the legend LEVANT and the medal is in bronze. The
following bars were issued in silver gilt: LEVANT
and LEVANT 1925-1926. It was later issued by the
Vichy government with the bar LEVANT 1941. Ribbon:
white and blue horizontal stripes   C

19. VICTORY MEDAL (MEDAILLE INTERALLIEE) 1914-18 (1922)

Bronze medal with Winged Victory on the obv. of the
usual type. Multicoloured ribbon as for the other
victory medals of WW I   B

20. MEDAILLE COMMEMORATIVE DU LIBAN (1926)

This medal was issued by the Lebanese government,
but essentially for issue to French troops who served
in that country at the time. Bronze with obv. a palm
with crossed swords and the legend in French and

Arabic <u>POUR LE LIBAN</u>. Ribbon: blue and red vertical
stripes   C

21.   <u>MEDAILLE D'ORIENT 1915-18</u> (1926)

Same design as No. 14 with the legend <u>ORIENT</u>,
<u>HONNEUR ET PATRIE</u> and the dates <u>1915-1918</u>. Ribbon:
blue with three yellow stripes. Bronze C

22.   <u>MEDAILLE DES DARDANELLES 1915-18</u> (1926)

Exactly the same but with <u>DARDANELLES</u> instead of
<u>ORIENT</u> and the ribbon is <u>white and green</u>   C

23.   <u>MEDAL FOR ESCAPED PRISONERS</u> (1926)

Bronze medal with obv. effigy of the Republic with
the legend <u>REPUBLIQUE FRANCAISE</u>; rev. legend <u>MEDAILLE</u>
<u>DES EVADES</u>. Ribbon: green with three red stripes   C

24.   <u>COMBATANT'S CROSS</u> (1930)

Bronze cross with obv. Republic's head with the
legend <u>REPUBLIQUE FRANCAISE</u> in a circle in the centre
of the cross and on the rev. legend <u>CROIX DU</u>
<u>COMBATTANT</u>. Ribbon: light blue with seven thin red
stripes. A similar cross was awarded by the Vichy
government in 1941 with the dates <u>1939-1940</u> and a
ribbon light blue with five black lines. Valuation
for either C

25.   <u>VOLUNTEER COMBATANT'S CROSS (CROIX DU COMBATTANT</u>
<u>VOLONTAIRE DE LA GUERRE 1914-1918)</u> (1935)

Bronze cross with helmeted soldier's head and sword
on the obv. and legend <u>CROIX DU COMBATTANT VOLONTAIRE</u>
<u>1914-1918</u> on the rev. Ribbon: green with a central
red stripe and yellow edges   C

26.   <u>VOLUNTARY MILITARY SERVICES CROSS (CROIX DES SERVICES</u>
<u>MILITAIRES VOLONTAIRES)</u> (1934)

Cross with the Republic's head and the legend
<u>REPUBLIQUE FRANCAISE</u> and on the rev. the legend

SERVICES MILITAIRES VOLONTAIRES. There are three
classes: (a) gold (b) silver (c) bronze. Ribbon:
light blue with red stripe for (c), with added white
edging for (b) and additionally a rosette for (a).
When issued to the air force, wings are added to
the medal, and for the navy, an anchor of the same
metal as the cross is worn on the ribbon.

  (a) and (b)   C

  (c)   B

27. MEDAILLE DE LA RESISTANCE FRANCAISE (1943)

Bronze circular medal with obv. a shield with the
Lorraine cross; rev. PATRIA NON IMMEMOR. The medal
is dated on the obv. XVIII VI MCMXL. Ribbon: black
with red stripes. Also awarded with a rosette on
the ribbon C

28. FREE FRENCH FORCES MEDAL

Silver Lorraine cross with the legend FRANCE LIBRE.
Ribbon: dark blue with diagonal red stripes B

29. MEDAILLE DE LA FRANCE LIBEREE (1947)

Bronze circular medal with a map of France with the
date 1944 in the centre and broken chains round on
the obv.; on the rev. the initials R.F., and the
legend LA FRANCE A SES LIBERATEURS. Ribbon: two
rainbows with the red on the edges B

30. WORLD WAR II COMMEMORATIVE MEDAL 1939-45

Obv. bronze oval-shaped medal with Gallic cock over
a Lorraine cross; on the rev. the legend REPUBLIQUE
FRANCAISE and the legend GUERRE 1939-1945. Ribbon:
blue with central Vs in red and green edge within
thin red stripes. The following bars, in white
metal, were awarded: FRANCE, NORVEGE, AFRIQUE,
LIBERATION, ALLEMAGNE, EXTREME-ORIENT, GRANDE-BRETAGNE,
U.R.S.S., ATLANTIQUE, MEDITERRANNEE, MANCHE, MER DU
NORD, DEFENCE PASSIVE, ENGAGE VOLONTAIRE. The bars
do not affect the value B

21 obv. GREAT BRITAIN, Crimea Medal 1854–6, with
'SEBASTOPOL' bar, silver

22 obv. GREAT BRITAIN, Turkish Medal for the Crimean War,
Sardinian type, silver

23 obv. GREAT BRITAIN, Indian General Service Medal 1854,
with bar 'BURMA 1885–7', silver

24 obv. GREAT BRITAIN, Egyptian Medal 1882–9, with bar
'SUAKIN 1885', silver

25 obv. GREAT BRITAIN, Queen's South Africa Medal
1899–1902, with five bars, silver

26 obv. GREAT BRITAIN, Volunteer Long Service Medal
1894–1930, Queen Victoria issue

27 obv. GREAT BRITAIN, Order of St John, Serving Brother's
badge, silver and enamel

28 obv. GREAT BRITAIN, St John Ambulance Brigade Long
Service Medal with two bars, silver issue

29 obv. GREAT BRITAIN, Queen Victoria Jubilee Medal, 1887
Metropolitan Police issue, bronze

30 rev. GREAT BRITAIN, Queen Victoria Jubilee Medal 1897,
London County Council Metropolitan Fire Brigade, bronze

31 obv. GREAT BRITAIN, King Edward VII Coronation Medal 1902, silver

32 obv. GREAT BRITAIN, King Edward VII Police Medal 1903 for Visit to Scotland, bronze

33 obv. GREAT BRITAIN, King George V, Coronation Medal 1911, Scottish Police issue, silver. (Note privately made suspension brooch in silver)

34 obv. GREAT BRITAIN, Royal Navy Long Service and Good Conduct Medal, King George V issue, Admiral's bust, silver

35 obv. GREAT BRITAIN, Territorial Efficiency Medal 1908–30, King George V issue, silver

36 obv. GREAT BRITAIN, Indian General Service Medal 1908–35, King George V issue, 1st type 1911–29 with bar 'AFGHANISTAN NWF 1919', silver, Calcutta Mint issue

37 obv. GREAT BRITAIN, do., but 2nd type 1930–6 with bar 'MOHMAND 1933', silver, Calcutta Mint issue

38 obv. GREAT BRITAIN, Military Medal, King George V Issue, 1st type, silver

39 obv. GREAT BRITAIN, British War Medal 1914–18, silver

40 obv. GREAT BRITAIN, Victory Medal 1914–18, bronze gilt

31. <u>MEDAL FOR THE ITALIAN CAMPAIGN OF 1943–4</u> (1953)

Silvered bronze medal with obv. Gallic cock with the
legend CORPS EXPEDITIONNAIRE FRANCAIS D'ITALIE
1943–1944. Rev. REPUBLIQUE FRANCAISE – C.E.F.
Ribbon: similar to No. 7   B

32. <u>INDO-CHINA CAMPAIGN MEDAL</u> (1953)

Bronze medal with three-headed elephant and snakes
with the legend INDOCHINE and REPUBLIQUE FRANCAISE
on the obv.; rev. CORPS EXPEDITIONNAIRE FRANCAIS
D'EXTREME ORIENT and wreath. The suspender is in the
shape of a dragon. Ribbon: green and yellow   B

33. <u>KOREAN WAR MEDAL</u> (1952)

Obv. arms of Korea on symbolic background; rev.
REPUBLIQUE FRANCAISE and MEDAILLE COMMEMORATIVE
FRANCAISE DES OPERATIONS DE L'ORGANISATION DES
NATIONS UNIES EN COREE. The medal is attached to the
ribbon by a suspender in the shape of a pagoda roof.
Ribbon: French and UN colours   B

34. <u>MEDAILLE DE MERITE DE L'AFRIQUE NOIRE</u> (1941)

Vichy government medal for issue to African troops
in French Equatorial Africa, Somaliland and Madagascar.
Bronze with obv. map of Africa; rev. anchor and
native characters. Ribbon: pale blue with thin green
and red stripes   B

35. <u>CROIX DE GUERRE DE LA LEGION VOLONTAIRE FRANCAISE</u>
(1942)

Issued by the Vichy government to French troops
fighting on the Russian front with the Germans.
Bronze with obv. French coat of arms over German
eagle; rev. legend CROIX DE GUERRE LEGIONNAIRE.
Ribbon: green with thin black stripes   E

36. <u>VERDUN MEDAL</u> (1916)

Issued by the town of Verdun. Bronze with obv.
soldier with fixed bayonet and field gun with the

legend <u>ON NE PASSE PAS</u>. Ribbon: red with tricolor
edging and a bronze bar is worn on the ribbon <u>VERDUN</u>
<u>21 FEVRIER 1916</u>   B

37. <u>MEDAILLE DE HAUTE-SILESIE</u> (1921) (Illustration No. 10)

Issued by the Allied government in Silesia. Bronze
with obv. eagle within a shield surrounded by oak
leaves with the legend above <u>HAUTE SILESIE</u>; rev.
legend <u>COMMISSION INTERRALLIEE DE GOUVERNEMENT ET DE</u>
<u>PLEBISCITE</u> with dates <u>1920-1922</u>. Ribbon: blue with
yellow central stripe   C

38. <u>MEDAILLE DE RHENANIE</u>

Semi-official medal issued to the French occupation
forces on the Rhine after WW II. Obv. feminine
allegorical head. Bronze. Ribbon: blue with red and
white stripes   B

39. <u>MEDAILLE COMMEMORATIVE FRANCAISE DES OPERATIONS AU</u>
<u>MOYEN ORIENT</u> (1957)

Bronze medal with obv. Republic's head with the
legend <u>REPUBLIQUE FRANCAISE</u>; rev. legend <u>MEDAILLE</u>
<u>COMMEMORATIVE DES OPERATIONS AU MOYEN ORIENT</u>.
<u>Ribbon: blue with three yellow vertical stripes</u>.
Bar <u>MOYEN ORIENT</u>   B

40. <u>MEDAILLE COMMEMORATIVE DES OPERATIONS DE SECURITE ET</u>
<u>DE MAINTIEN DE L'ORDRE</u> (1958)

Obv. similar to No. 39; rev. legend <u>MEDAILLE</u>
<u>COMMEMORATIVE OPERATIONS DE SECURITE ET MAINTIEN DE</u>
<u>L'ORDRE</u> within a wreath. Bronze. Ribbon: white and
red vertical stripes with broad central blue stripe.
Bar <u>ALGERIE</u>   B

41. <u>MILITARY VALOUR CROSS (CROIX DE LA VALEUR MILITAIRE)</u>
(1956)

Bronze cross with obv. Republic's head with legend
<u>REPUBLIQUE FRANCAISE</u> and on the rev. legend <u>CROIX DE</u>
<u>LA VALEUR MILITAIRE</u>. Ribbon: red with one broad and
two narrow white stripes   B

66

42. <u>MEDAL FOR CHINA CAMPAIGN 1900-1</u> (Illustration No. 19)

Circular medal in silver. Obv. Republic head with
legend <u>REPUBLIQUE FRANCAISE</u>; rev. trophy or arms
and legend <u>CHINE 1900-1901</u>. With or without bar
<u>CHINE 1900-1901</u>. Ribbon: green and orange stripes C

GERMANY

Up to and including the WW I, there had been so many
orders, decorations and medals issued by the various
independent German states that they are beyond the
scope of this book, in which only the awards of the
unified Germany are listed. There are, however, two
exceptions: Pour le Merite and the Iron Cross, as
these, although they started as Prussian orders were
generally used.

1. <u>POUR LE MERITE</u> (1810)

Although established earlier, it was only in 1810
that it became a military order, to which a civil
division was added later. Maltese cross in blue
enamel, with gold edges, with four golden eagles
between the arms of the cross. On the upper arm of
the cross, a crown above the letter F (for Frederick
I of Prussia), on the remaining three the words
<u>POUR – LE ME – RITE</u> in gold. The order is worn round
the neck and the ribbon is black and white and silver
stripes towards the edges   J

A higher class of the order is worn with three
golden oak leaves on the ring for suspension, and
the ribbon has an additional central silver
stripe   K

Copies of the insignia vary in value according to
the quality of the workmanship and the metals
used   D–F

2. <u>THE IRON CROSS</u> (1813)

The Iron Cross was not a permanent award, but only
issued for specific wars: (a) The Freedom War of
1813 (b) Franco-German War of 1870-1 (c) World War I

and (d) World War II.

<u>(a)   1813 Iron Cross</u>

   (i)   breast star of the Grand Cross of the Iron
         Cross. A solid-gold star with eight points;
         only one was issued and destroyed in the
         last century.

  (ii)   Grand Cross - cast-iron cross with silver
         rim. Obv. plain; rev. Prussian crown, the
         royal cipher F.W. (Friedrich Wilhelm III)
         at the top, three oak leaves in the centre
         and the date 1813 at the bottom. Worn
         round the neck with insignia larger than
         that of 1st Cl. (65mm instead of 40mm).
         Only a few were issued and these are
         extremely rare   no recent valuation

 (iii)   1st Cl. There have been several types, some
         in cloth, but the main one is in iron with
         silver rim, of similar design to (ii)
         above, but with rings soldered at the
         corners of each arm of the cross for sewing
         to the uniform and a small dia. (about
         40mm)   J

  (iv)   2nd Cl. Is similar to 1st Cl., often smaller
         (28 to 40mm) and worn from a black ribbon
         with two white stripes for combatant troops
         (the reverse for non-combatant troops).
         There are many slight variations of design,
         mounting and ribbon for this award.
         Generally the valuation is   I

<u>(b)   1870 Iron Cross</u>

   (i)   Grand Cross - same design as the 1813 issue
         but with royal cipher W (Wilhelm I) and
         date 1870 on the obv. Instead of being
         plain, whilst the rev. is like the original
         1813 issue's obv. There are slight
         variations of design and fewer than ten
         were awarded. These are extremely rare
                          no recent valuation

70

(ii)   1st Cl. Obv. King's crown on the upper arm,
       W̲ in the centre and 1̲8̲7̲0̲ on the lower arm.
       Plain silver rev. with pin for attachment.
       Usually slightly larger than the 1813
       type   H

(iii) 2nd Cl. Same obv. as the 1st Cl., but with
       rev. as the 1813 cross 2nd Cl. The cross
       is suspended from the same ribbon as the
       1813 issue. Combatant and non-combatant
       ribbons were again issued   E

(c)   25th Anniversary Oak Leaves (1895) - Recipients
of the 1870 Iron Cross alive in 1895 were entitled
to wear an emblem of three oak leaves in white metal
with the fig 25 either above the 1st Cl. cross on
the uniform, or in the case of the 2nd Cl. cross, on
its ribbon. 1870 Iron Crosses with this emblem are
a little more valuable than without.

(d)   1914 Iron Cross

(i)   Grand Cross. Similar to (b) (i) but with
       the date 1̲9̲1̲4̲ instead of 1̲8̲7̲0̲ on the obv.;
       the rev. remains the same. There are
       various types of this cross some with the
       stamp 900 on the rev. to indicate the
       silver content. Only a few were awarded
       and they are extremely rare. One breast
       star of the Grand Cross of the Iron Cross
       was also awarded.

(ii)   1st Cl. Similar to the 1870 issue but with
       date 1̲9̲1̲4̲ in the lower arm. There are
       numerous variations of this cross: some
       have a pin at the back, others a screw
       type of fastener. Some have a silver
       content mark 800. Two types of ribbon as
       before   C

(iii) 2nd Cl. As the 1870 issue but with the
       date 1̲9̲1̲4̲ on the obv. Same ribbons. Again
       there are many different variations of
       this cross, and some are stamped with the
       silver content, whilst others are in metal
       other than silver   B

(iv)   A clasp was awarded from 1915 to holders of
       the 1870 Iron Cross who earned the Iron
       Cross again, and the clasp was a small
       white metal replica of the 1914 cross. It
       was worn above the 25th Anniversary Oak
       Leaves. Genuine specimens are rare
                             no recent valuation

<u>(e)   1939-45 Iron Cross</u> - Design remains the same as
previously, except that there is now a swastika and
the date <u>1939</u> on the obv.

       (i)   Grand Cross. Twice the size of the 2nd Cl.
             and is worn round the neck on a black,
             white and red ribbon. It is in cast iron
             and silver and stamped 900 on the rev. to
             indicate the silver content. Only one was
             issued and destroyed in the war. Copies
             exist, with various slight variations.

      (ii)   breast star to the Grand Cross, eight-
             pointed gold star with the 1st Cl. Iron
             Cross superimposed. It is in doubt whether
             it was ever issued.

     (iii)   Knight's Cross of the Iron Cross. Similar
             to (i), but smaller and also worn round
             the neck. A few of these were awarded with
             Oak Leaves, Swords, Diamonds and Golden
             Oak Leaves, the latter being the rarest.
             Without any additional emblems   E

             If genuine insignia with genuine emblems
             which can be verified, the value is H-J,
             depending on the details of the award.

      (iv)   1st Cl. Obv. iron and silver cross, with
             the swastika and <u>1939</u>; the rev. is plain,
             with a vertical pin for attachment. Screw-
             back types are less common   C

       (v)   2nd Cl. Iron Cross. Obv. same as the 1st
             Cl., but with the date <u>1813</u> on the rev.
             Suspended from a black, white and red
             ribbon. Some crosses have 800 stamped on
             the ring to indicate silver content   B

72

(f) Denazified Iron Crosses (1957) - Those who have
earned the 1939-45 Iron Cross are entitled to wear
the denazified version issued in 1957, which is the
same design except that three oak leaves with acorns
replace the swastika. The Grand Cross has not been
redesigned.

    (i) Knight's Cross with or without
          emblems   E

    (ii) 1st Cl. and 2nd Cl.   C

3.   CROSS OF HONOUR (1934)

Bronzed iron cross. Obv. a shield with the dates
1914-1918 and laurels, with crossed swords, for
combatant troops and without for non-combatant.
Ribbon: black, white and red vertical stripes. The
lacquered iron version was issued to relatives of
dead recipients   C

4.   SERVICE MEDAL (1936)

A long-service and good-conduct award with a light-
blue ribbon.

    (a) gold cross for twenty-five years   C

    (b) silver cross for eighteen years   C

    (c) bronze medal for twelve years   B

    (d) frosted silver for four years   B

5.   BLOOD ORDER

Silver circular medal with obv. an eagle with wreath
and the date 9 NOV and the legend MUNCHEN 1913-1933;
rev. Feldherrnhalle in Munich, with a rayed swastika
above and the legend UND IHR HABT DOCH GESIEGT.
Ribbon: broad central red stripe with narrow white
and black ones at the edges   C

6.   GERMAN CROSS 1939-45

The most senior order issued during WW II in the
shape of large star with a rayed swastika in the

centre, and worn without ribbon. Three classes:

    (a) gold with brilliants   H
    (b) gold   F
    (c) silver   D

7.   <u>WAR MERIT CROSS 1939-45</u> (Illustrations Nos. 7, 8
     and 9)

     A junior type of Iron Cross.

     (a) 1st Cl. - silver cross with swastika in
          the obv. centre and <u>1939</u> on the rev. No
          ribbon; worn from a <u>pin</u> at the back.
          Issued with swords to combatant troops,
          and the swords appear between the arms of
          the cross - or without swords to non-
          combatants   C

     (b) 2nd Cl. - as (a) in bronze, but worn from
          a ribbon with a wide black centre stripe
          and narrower red and white ones on the
          edges   B

     (c) War Merit Medal - circular bronze medal.
          Obv. reproduction of the cross; rev.
          legend <u>FUR KRIEGSVERDIENST 1939</u>. The
          ribbon the same as for the 2nd Cl. cross
          but has a thin red stripe in the
          centre   B

8.   <u>CROSS OF HONOUR FOR THE SPANISH CAMPAIGN 1936</u>

     Similar design to the previous award, and worn
     without a ribbon, like the star of an order. Issued
     in gold with brilliants, gold, silver and bronze.
     No recent valuation for the first two classes, but
     silver cross D and bronze cross C

9.   <u>ENTRY INTO AUSTRIA MEDAL 1938</u>

     Circular silver medal. Obv. two allegorical figures
     representing Germany and Austria with a banner.
     Dated 13 March 1938. Ribbon: red with black and white
     edges B

10. ENTRY INTO CZECHOSLOVAKIA MEDAL 1938

Circular silver medal with similar design as the
previous one and dated 1 October 1938. Ribbon: equal
stripes of black, red and black with narrow white
edges   B

The same medal exists with a bronze ribbon bar to
commemorate the occupation of Bohemia and Moravia in
1939   C

11. MEDAL FOR THE CAMPAIGN IN RUSSIA 1941-2

Circular silver medal. Obv. Nazi eagle on a swastika
with a steel helmet and hand grenade on the upper
part of the medal; rev. legend WINTERSCHLACHT IM
OSTEN 1941/2 with crossed sword and laurel branch.
Ribbon: red with thin central black stripe and white
edging on each side   B

12. WEST WALL MEDAL

Oval bronze medal. Obv. eagle and swastika, crossed
sword and spade, and fortifications; rev., legend
FUR ARBEIT ZUM SCHUTZE DEUTSCHLAND. Ribbon: light
brown with two white stripes   B

13. MEDAL FOR THE RETURN OF MEMEL 1939

Circular silver medal similar to Nos. 9 and 10,
dated 22 March 1939. Ribbon: red and white with
central green vertical stripe   B

14. MEDAL FOR AFRICAN CAMPAIGN 1940-3

Bronze circular medal with obv. two knights in armour
standing on a crocodile; rev. archway with the
Italian fasces on one side and the swastika on the
other. Legend in Italian and German GERMAN-ITALIAN
CAMPAIGN IN AFRICA. Ribbon: black, white, red and
green. Intended for issue both in Germany and
Italy   B

Although, as already mentioned, the German states
are omitted, some of the Prussian medals most

commonly met are now listed:

15. <u>WAR WITH AUSTRIA 1866</u>

Bronze cross with legend <u>DER MAIN ARMEE, 1866</u>   C

16. <u>FRANCO-PRUSSIAN WAR MEDAL 1870-1</u>

Combatant and non-combatant issues B with bars
<u>METZ</u>, <u>GRAVELOTTE-ST.PRIVAT</u>, <u>COLOMBEY-NEUILLY</u>,
<u>SPICHEREN</u>, <u>BEAUMONT</u>, <u>SEDAN</u>, <u>ST. QUENTIN</u>, <u>PARIS</u>, etc.
Usually found with several bars   C

17. <u>CHINA CAMPAIGN MEDAL 1900</u>

White metal   C

18. <u>SOUTH-WEST AFRICA CAMPAIGN 1904-6</u> (Illustration No. 6)

Bronze gilt. Obv. helmeted figure of Germania with
legend <u>SUDWEST AFRICA - 1904-06</u>; rev. <u>W II</u> under
crown with crossed swords underneath, and legend
<u>DEN SIEGREICHCHEN STREITERN</u>. Ribbon: vertical black
and white stripes with short horizontal red ones in
the centre. Also awarded with clasp <u>KALAHARI 1908</u>
Either   C

GREAT BRITAIN

1. <u>MOST NOBLE ORDER OF THE GARTER</u> (1348)

      (a) garter (dark-blue velvet and gold)   G

      (b) collar, gold and enamel
                               no recent valuation

      (c) the George (St George), suspended from
           the collar   no recent valuation

      (d) badge or Lesser George, worn on
           the sash   K

      (e) star, embroidered   I

      (f) star, metal   L

Because so few of these items are available for sale,
it is difficult to price them exactly. The above
valuations are for the cheapest items, but earlier
models, or insignia belonging to a well-known
personality, or when sold at an auction, might well
fetch much higher prices.

2. <u>MOST ANCIENT AND NOBLE ORDER OF THE THISTLE</u> (1687)

      (a) collar, gold and enamel
                             no recent valuation

      (b) badge or jewel, gold and enamel   L

      (c) star, silver and enamel   K

      (d) star, embroidered   I

      (e) sash badge   K

Same remarks as above for the Garter.

3.   <u>MOST ILLUSTRIOUS ORDER OF ST PATRICK</u> (1783)

      (a) collar, gold and enamel
                                    no recent valuation

      (b) badge, suspended from the collar, gold
           and enamel   L

      (c) star, silver and enamel   K

      (d) star, embroidered   H

4.   <u>MOST HONOURABLE ORDER OF THE BATH</u> (1725)

      (a) Knight Grand Cross star and gold
           badge   K

      (b) do., star only (metal)   I

      (c) star, embroidered   F

      (d) sash badge, silver and enamel   J

      (e) Knight Commander, metal star   I

      (f) do., embroidered   F

      (g) do., neck badge, silver and enamel J

      (h) Companion, neck badge, silver and
           enamel   I

      (i) do., breast badge, silver and
           enamel   F

The civil division insignia is different in design
and usually worth less.

5.   <u>MOST DISTINGUISHED ORDER OF ST MICHAEL AND ST GEORGE</u>
      (1818)

      (a) Knight Grand Cross, collar chain   K

      (b) do., star   I

      (c) do., sash badge, silver and enamel I

      (d) Knight Commander, star   I

      (e) do., neck badge, silver and enamel H

      (f) Companion, breast badge, silver and
           enamel   G

      (g) do., neck badge, silver and enamel G

6.   <u>ORDER OF MERIT</u> (1902)

Military division only. Civil division insignia
worth less.

       (a)   Edward VII   L

       (b)   George V   L

       (c)   George VI   L

       (d)   Elizabeth II   L

7.   <u>ROYAL VICTORIAN ORDER</u> (1896)

       (a)   Knight Grand Cross collar chain
                                no value available

       (b)   do., badge and star   J

       (c)   Knight Commander, neck badge and breast
           star   I

       (d)   Commander, neck badge   G

       (e)   Member, 4th Cl., breast badge,
           enamel   E

       (f)   Member, 5th Cl., breast badge,
           frosted silver   E

The insignia are numbered on the rev.

8.   <u>ROYAL VICTORIAN MEDAL</u>

	<u>Silver gilt</u>	<u>Silver</u>	<u>Bronze</u>
Victoria	D	D	D
Edward VII	D	D	D
George V	D	D	D
George VI	D	D	—
Elizabeth II	D	D	—

(Edward VII insignia is at the top end of the
bracket, Victoria at the lowest.)

9. <u>ORDER OF THE BRITISH EMPIRE</u> (1917) (Illustration
    No. 48)

The insignia of the two divisions, military and civil,
are the same, but the ribbon of the military division
has a narrow stripe in the centre and is generally
more valuable than the civil one. Insignia for a
woman worth more than for a man, particularly in the
military division. Two types: (a) 1917 to 1936,
Britannia in the centre of stars and badges, and (b)
after 1936 conjointed busts of George V and Queen
Mary.

		<u>1st type</u>	<u>2nd type</u>
(a)	Knight Grand Cross, sash badge and star	I	J
(b)	Knight Commander, neck badge and star	H	I
(c)	Commander, neck badge	E	F
(d)	Officer, breast badge, silver gilt	D	D
(e)	Member, breast badge, silver	C	D

Ribbon: originally purple with narrow scarlet stripe
in the centre for the military division, altered in
1936 to rose pink with pearl-grey stripe.

10. <u>BRITISH EMPIRE MEDAL</u> (1917)

(a)	1st type (until 1922), George V	D
(b)	2nd type, George V	
(i)	the Medal of the Order of the British Empire for Gallantry (EGM)	I
(ii)	the Medal of the Order of the British Empire for Meritorious Service	D
(c)	do., George VI (i) (until 1940)	I
	George VI (ii)	D

80

(d) Elizabeth II for Meritorious Service D
     do., with Gallantry Emblem (Forces)   F

Ribbon: the same as for the Order of the British
Empire but narrower. There is also a military and a
civil division. The prices above are for the military-
division awards.

11. <u>ORDER OF THE COMPANION OF HONOUR</u> (1917)

Oval-shaped gold badge with the legend <u>IN ACTION
FAITHFUL AND IN HONOUR CLEAR</u>. Ribbon: <u>carmine with
gold thread</u>   K

12. <u>DISTINGUISHED SERVICE ORDER</u> (1886)

     (a) Victoria, gold   J

     (b) do., silver gilt   G

     (c) Edward VII   I

     (d) George V   G

     (e) George VI, 1st type   G

     (f) do., 2nd type   I

     (g) Elizabeth II   I

13. <u>VICTORIA CROSS</u> (1856)

Bronze cross pattee, with crown and lion in the
centre and the inscription <u>FOR VALOUR</u>, suspended from
a <u>V</u> to a bar. The name, rank and unit of the recipient
is engraved on the back of this bar. The ribbon was
originally blue for the navy and crimson for the army;
since WW I it has been purple for all three services.

    It is difficult to give a value to this
decoration as much depends on the citation and the
campaign. It can be said that post-1918 awards are
rarer than the earlier ones, and those to the Royal
Air Force fewer than to the other services   L
Copies, depending on how well they are made, sell
for   C

14. <u>GEORGE CROSS</u> (1940)

Plain silver cross with St George and the dragon,
and the inscription <u>FOR GALLANTRY</u> in the centre of
the cross. Suspended from a straight bar suspender.
The rev. is plain and bears the name of the recipient
and date of award. It can be awarded to both civilians
and members of the forces; the prices indicated are
for the latter, which are more valuable. Holders of
the Medal of the Order of the British Empire for
Gallantry in 1940 could exchange it for the George
Cross, and these exchange awards are worth less than
those made later. Ribbon: plain blue.

  (a) exchange awards K

  (b) awards since 1940 L

15. <u>GEORGE MEDAL</u> (1940)

Circular medal in silver with the sovereign's head on
the obv. and St George and the dragon on the rev.,
with the legend <u>THE GEORGE MEDAL</u>. Ribbon: red with
thin blue vertical stripes. Military awards H

16. <u>ROYAL RED CROSS</u>

  (a) 1st Cl., Victoria, gold and enamel G
     do., silver gilt and enamel E

  (b) 1st Cl., Edward VII, gold and
     enamel G

  (c) 1st Cl., George V, silver gilt and
     enamel D

  (d) 1st Cl., George VI, silver gilt and
     enamel D

  (e) 1st Cl., Elizabeth II, silver gilt
     and enamel D

  (f) 2nd Cl., George V, silver and enamel C

  (g) do., George VI, silver and enamel D

  (h) do., Elizabeth II, silver and enamel D

Ribbon: blue with two red vertical stripes on the
edges.

17. <u>DISTINGUISHED SERVICE CROSS</u> (1901)

Called the Conspicuous Service Cross until its name
was changed in 1914, it was a naval award. Plain
silver cross pattee with the cipher of the reigning
sovereign on the obv. surmounted by a crown. Rev. is
plain. There were only eight CSCs issued and these
are very rare. The prices quoted are for the later
DSCs.

    (a) George V   F

    (b) George VI, 1st type   F

    (c) do., 2nd type, G vi R   I

    (d) Elizabeth II   I

Ribbon: dark blue with a white stripe in the centre.

18. <u>MILITARY CROSS</u> (1914)

Ornamental silver cross with a crown on each arm and
the royal cipher in the centre. This is a military
award which can be granted to the air force for
service on the ground. Ribbon: white with purple
stripe in the centre.

    (a) George V (WW I period) without bar   D
                                  with bar   G

    (b) do., awards in the period 1918-36   I

    (c) George VI, 1st type   F

    (d) do., 2nd type, G vi R   H

    (e) Elizabeth II   I

19. <u>DISTINGUISHED FLYING CROSS</u> (1918)

Silver ornate cross with the letters RAF surmounted
by a crown in the centre. Rev. royal cipher with the
date <u>1918</u>.

    (a) George V   H

    (b) George VI, 1st type   G

(c)	2nd type	G
(d)	Elizabeth II	I

Ribbon: violet and white diagonal stripes.

20. <u>AIR FORCE CROSS</u> (1918)

Ornate silver cross with the royal cipher on the ends
of each arm; Hermes in the centre of the cross. The
cross is surmounted by a crown. Rev. royal cipher with
the date <u>1918</u>

(a)	George V	H
(b)	George VI, 1st type	H
(c)	do., 2nd type, G vi R	I
(d)	Elizabeth II	I

Ribbon: crimson and white diagonal stripes.

21. <u>DISTINGUISHED CONDUCT MEDAL</u> (1854)

Silver circular medal. Obv. effigy of the reigning
sovereign; rev. legend <u>FOR DISTINGUISHED CONDUCT IN
THE FIELD</u>

(a)	Victoria	F
(b)	Edward VII	F
(c)	George V, pre-1930	E
	1930-6	H
(d)	George VI	G
(e)	Elizabeth II	H

Ribbon: purple with a blue stripe in the centre.

22. <u>CONSPICUOUS GALLANTRY MEDAL</u> (ROYAL NAVY) (1855)

Circular silver medal with obv. effigy of the
reigning sovereign; rev. legend <u>FOR CONSPICUOUS
GALLANTRY.</u>

| (a) | Victoria | J |

84

    (b) Edward VII   K

    (c) George V   J

    (d) George VI   J

    (e) Elizabeth II   no valuation

Ribbon: until 1921 blue, white and blue stripes of equal width; since, white with two narrow blue edges.

23. <u>CONSPICUOUS GALLANTRY MEDAL</u> (ROYAL AIR FORCE) (1943)

Same design, but the ribbon is light blue with dark-blue edges.

    (a) George VI   K

    (b) Elizabeth II   no valuation

24. <u>DISTINGUISHED SERVICE MEDAL</u> (ROYAL NAVY) (1914)

Circular silver medal with obv. the effigy of the reigning sovereign; rev. legend <u>FOR DISTINGUISHED SERVICE</u>, surmounted by a crown and within a wreath.

    (a) George V, 1914–30, uncrowned head   E

    (b) do., 1930–7, crowned head   J

    (c) George VI, 1938–49, 1st type   E

    (d) do., 1949–53, 2nd type, without
        <u>INDIAE IMP</u>   H

    (e) Elizabeth II   no valuation

Ribbon: blue, white and blue with narrow blue stripe in the centre.

25. <u>MILITARY MEDAL</u> (1916)

Silver circular medal. Ribbon: blue, white and red vertical stripes. Obv. effigy of the reigning sovereign; rev. legend <u>FOR BRAVERY IN THE FIELD</u>.

    (a) George V, 1st type, 1916–30 (Illustration
        No. 38)
        without bar   C
        with bar   E

    (b)   do., 2nd type, crowned head 1930-8   H

    (c)   George VI, 1st type, 1938-48   F

    (d)   do., 2nd type, 1948-53 without INDIAE
           IMP   G

    (e)   Elizabeth II, 1953-8, BR OMN in
           legend   H

    (f)   do., from 1958, without BR OMN in
           legend   I

26. DISTINGUISHED FLYING MEDAL (1918)

Oval-shaped silver medal with obv. effigy of the
reigning sovereign; rev. Athena Nike sitting on an
aeroplane with a hawk and the legend FOR COURAGE.

    (a)   George V, 1st type, 1918-30   H

    (b)   do., 2nd type, 1930-8, crowned head   I

    (c)   George VI, 1st type, with IND IMP,
           1938-49   G

    (d)   do., 2nd type, without IND IMP,
           1949-53   I

    (e)   Elizabeth II   J

Ribbon: diagonal violet and white stripes. Originally
these were horizontal.

27. AIR FORCE MEDAL (1918)

Oval-shaped silver medal, similar to above, but rev.
shows Hermes on a hawk bestowing a wreath. The
ribbon is similar but with crimson instead of violet
stripes.

    (a)   George V, 1st type   I

    (b)   do., 2nd type   I

    (c)   George VI, 1st type   H

    (d)   do., 2nd type   I

    (e)   Elizabeth II   I

28. <u>NAVAL GOLD MEDAL 1795–1815</u>

Two sizes: large 2in dia. and small 1.3in dia. Obv.
an antique galley with Victory placing a wreath on
Britannia's head and the Union shield; rev. name of
the recipient and battle for which the medal was
awarded. The medal hangs from a plain gold ring and
was worn round the neck with a ribbon in white with
blue borders. These medals are all very rare   L

29. <u>NAVAL GENERAL SERVICE MEDAL 1793–1840</u> (1848)

Obv. Victoria young head with legend <u>VICTORIA REGINA</u>
and the date <u>1848</u>; rev. Britannia seated on a sea
horse. Circular silver medal hanging from a plain-
bar suspension, from a white ribbon with blue edges.

   This medal covers a wide range of naval actions
and 230 bars bearing the name of a naval action, the
the name of a vessel winning an engagement or the
words <u>BOAT SERVICE</u>, with a date, were issued. The
medal was not issued until 1848 and only to the
survivors of the actions in question, so in some
cases the number of recipients is very small. Values
depend very much on the bars or combinations of bars,
the rank of the recipient and the action; they are
often offered at auctions and the price can vary a
great deal from one sale to the next, depending on
interest at the time. Valuations for the most common
bars are:

    (a)   <u>SYRIA</u>   F

    (b)   <u>ALGIERS</u>   G

    (c)   <u>NAVARINO</u>   F

    (d)   <u>TRAFALGAR</u> (although there are more than
          <u>1,700 of</u> these, they are very much sought
          after)   I

    (e)   <u>BASQUE ROADS</u>   H

    (f)   <u>MARTINIQUE</u>   H

    (g)   <u>GUADALOUPE</u>   H

The majority of the other bars are in the valuation
brackets I, J and K.

30. <u>ARMY GOLD MEDALS AND CROSSES 1806-14</u>

Obv. some with the effigy of George III with the
legend <u>GEORGIUS TERTIUS REX</u>; others with Britannia
seated holding a laurel leaf. The crosses had a lion
in the centre, were shaped like a Maltese cross and
had the name of a battle on each arm of the cross.
There were small gold medals (1.3in dia.), large
gold ones (2in dia.) and gold crosses - with or
without bars. The small gold medals without bars or
with one or two bars are the cheapest, being valued
at K; the remainder are in the L bracket. Ribbon:
crimson with blue edges.

31. <u>MILITARY GENERAL SERVICE MEDAL 1793-1814</u> (1848)

Obv. Victoria young head with the legend <u>VICTORIA
REGINA</u> and date <u>1848</u>; rev. Queen Victoria standing
on a dais crowning with a laurel wreath the figure
of the Duke of Wellington kneeling. Legend <u>TO THE
BRITISH ARMY</u> and dates <u>1793-1814</u>. There are twenty-
nine different bars to this medal: <u>EGYPT</u>, <u>MAIDA</u>,
<u>ROLEIA</u>, <u>VIMIERA</u>, <u>SAHAGUN AND BENEVENTE</u>, <u>CORUNNA</u>,
<u>MARTINIQUE</u>, <u>TALAVERA</u>, <u>GUADALOUPE</u>, <u>BUSACO</u>, <u>BARROSA</u>,
<u>FUENTES D'ONOR</u>, <u>ALBUHERA</u>, <u>JAVA</u>, <u>CIUDAD RODRIGO</u>,
<u>BADAJOZ</u>, <u>SALAMANCA</u>, <u>VITTORIA</u>, <u>PYRENEES</u>, <u>ST. SEBASTIAN</u>,
<u>NIVELLE</u>, <u>NIVE</u>, <u>ORTHES</u> and <u>TOULOUSE</u> are the cheapest -
in the F bracket on average.   <u>SAHAGUN</u> is valued at
H, and the rarer bars: <u>BENEVENTE</u>, <u>FORT DETROIT</u>,
<u>CHATEAUGUAY</u>, <u>CHRYSTLER'S FARM</u> are <u>J</u>

Here again a great deal depends on the holder, his
rank, his unit, and in some cases a medal with a
single bar is more valuable than one with multiple
bars. As an indication, these are the valuations for
the cheapest multiple-bar medals:

        2 bars   F
        3 bars   G
        4 bars   G
        5 bars   G
        6 bars   H
        7 bars   H
        8 bars   I
        9 bars   I

```
10 bars    I
11 bars    I
12 bars    J
13 bars    J
```

Ribbon: crimson with blue edges

32. <u>WATERLOO MEDAL 1815</u> (1816)

Circular silver medal with clip steel ring. Often
found with privately made silver suspender. Obv.
effigy of the Prince Regent with the legend GEORGE
P. REGENT; rev. Victory seated on a plinth. Legend
WELLINGTON and WATERLOO JUNE 18th 1815. The value of
this medal is greatly influenced by the unit as well
as the rank of the holder. Less glamourous units are
in the bracket G and the Guards, Light and Heavy
Cavalry in the bracket H; those to officers and
senior NCOs are at the top end of the bracket.
Ribbon: crimson with blue edges.

33. <u>FIRST INDIA MEDAL 1799-1826</u> (1851)

Issued by the Honourable East India Company. Obv.
Queen Victoria young head with legend VICTORIA REGINA;
rev. seated figure of Winged Victory with legend THE
ARMY OF INDIA and the dates 1799-1826. The medals
issued to Europeans have the name impressed and more
valuable than those issued to native troops which
were engraved. The rarer bars are more valuable singly
than in combination. There are twenty-one bars, the
most common being: AVA, BHURTPOOR G; then NEPAUL,
POONA, KIRKEE AND POONA, NAGPORE, SEETABULDEE AND
NAGPORE, MAHEIDPOOR H; most of the remainder,
ALLIGHUR, BATTLE OF DELHI, ASSYE, ASSEERGHUR,
LASWARREE, GAWILGHUR, ARGAUM, DATTLE OF DEIG, CAPTURE
OF DEIG, are I-J. Finally, DEFENCE OF DELHI, KIRKEE,
SEETABULDEE and CORYGAUM are all rare and estimated
K-L

     The prices indicated are for medals with
impressed names, those with engraved names, to native
troops, which are difficult to verify, would be
cheaper. Please note that the prices indicated are

the lowest for these bars, which means that they may
well be in some cases in a two- or three-bar
combination.

34.   <u>MEDAL FOR THE CAPTURE OF GHUZNEE 1839</u>

Circular silver medal with a crimson and green
ribbon with obv. gateway of the Ghuznee fortress
with the word <u>GHUZNEE</u> on a scroll below; rev. two
branches of laurel with a mural crown inside and the
legend <u>23rd JULY</u> above and <u>1839</u> below.

    (a)   issued to British troops   F

    (b)   issued to Indian troops   E

35.   <u>JELLALABAD MEDAL</u> (1842)

Obv. effigy of Queen Victoria with the legend
<u>VICTORIA VINDEX</u>; rev. winged figure of Victory flying
over the Jellalabad fortress with the legend
<u>JELLALABAD VII APRIL</u> and below, the date <u>MDCCCXLII</u>.

A Jellalabad medal without the effigy of Queen
Victoria and with a mural crown on the obv. has
been issued previously and the above-mentioned medal
was meant to replace it. However, the first medal
was preferred and many recipients did not apply for
the later medal which is therefore rarer.

    (a)   1st type, mural crown   F

    (b)   2nd type, Queen Victoria   I

Ribbon: pink merging into yellow, and yellow into
blue.

36.   <u>CANDAHAR, GHUZNEE AND CABUL MEDALS 1842</u>

Obv. effigy of Victoria with the legend <u>VICTORIA</u>
<u>VINDEX</u>; rev. four types:

    (a)   crown with <u>CANDAHAR</u> and the date <u>1842</u>   H

    (b)   crown with <u>GHUZNEE</u> and <u>CABUL</u> in a
         laurel wreath and date <u>1842</u>   H

(c) as (a) above, but with <u>CANDAHAR</u>, <u>GHUZNEE</u>
     and <u>CABUL</u>   G

(d) as (a) but with <u>CABUL</u> only   F

37. MEDAL FOR THE DEFENCE OF KELAT-I-GHILZIE 1842

Obv. a shield bearing the name <u>KELAT-I-GHILZIE</u>,
surmounted by a mural crown and encircled by wreaths
of laurels; rev. trophy of arms with the word
<u>INVICTA</u> on a tablet and the date <u>MDCCCXLII</u>. Ribbon:
red, yellow and blue.

(a) European troops   J

(b) Indian troops   I

38. SCINDE CAMPAIGN MEDALS 1843

Obv. Queen Victoria with the legend <u>VICTORIA REGINA</u>;
rev. three different ones:

(a) laurel wreath surrounding a crown with
     <u>MEEANEE</u> and the date <u>1843</u>   I

(b) do., but <u>HYDERABAD</u> instead of <u>MEEANEE</u> G

(c) do., but with both names   H

39. STARS FOR THE GWALIOR CAMPAIGN 1843

Bronze stars made from guns captured during the
Gwalior Campaign of 1843. Obv. six-pointed bronze
star, 2in dia. with small silver star in the centre
on which the legends <u>MAHARAJPOOR 1843</u> or <u>PUNNIAR</u>
<u>1843</u> and the date 29th Dec. appear; rev. plain, with
name and regiment of the recipient engraved.
Originally issued with hooks, later fitted with
suspension clasps or rings to wear with a ribbon.
Either   F

40. <u>CHINA MEDAL</u> (1842)

Circular silver medal with obv. effigy of Queen
Victoria; rev. palm tree, oval shield with royal arms
and a trophy of weapons with legend <u>ARMIS EXPOSCERE</u>
PACEM CHINA and date <u>1842</u>. Ribbon: crimson with
yellow edges   F

41. <u>MEDAL FOR SUTLEJ CAMPAIGN 1845-6</u>

Obv. effigy of Queen Victoria; rev. Victory holding
a laurel wreath with the legend <u>ARMY OF THE SUTLEJ</u>
and at the bottom the name and date of the battle
for which the medal was issued. Further engagements
are indicated by a bar.

(a)	medal inscribed <u>MOODKEE 1845</u>, no bar	E
(b)	do., 1 bar	F
(c)	do., 2 bars	F
(d)	do., 3 bars	G
(e)	medal inscribed <u>FEROZESHUHUR 1845</u>, no bar	E
(f)	do., 1 bar	F
(g)	do., 2 bars	no recent valuation
(h)	medal inscribed <u>ALIWAL 1846</u>, no bar	E
(i)	do., 1 bar	F
(j)	medal inscribed SOBRAON 1846, no bar	E

42. <u>NEW ZEALAND MEDAL 1845-8</u>

Obv. Queen Victoria with diadem, legend <u>VICTORIA D :
G : BRITT : REG : F : D :</u>; rev. legend <u>NEW ZEALAND</u>
and <u>VIRTUTIS HONOR</u> and laurel wreath in which are
the date or dates when applicable.

(a)	undated	D
(b)	1845-6	H
(c)	1845-7	H
(d)	1846-7	G
(e)	1846	I
(f)	1847	I
(g)	1848	J

43. <u>PUNJAB CAMPAIGN MEDAL 1848-9</u>

Obv. effigy of Queen Victoria; rev. General Sir

Walter Raleigh Gilbert on horseback with a party of
Sikhs laying down their arms. Legend <u>TO THE ARMY OF
THE PUNJAB</u> and the date <u>MDCCCXLIX</u>. Issued without
bar or with up to two of the following: <u>MOOLTAN</u>,
<u>CHILIANWALA, GOOJERAT</u>.

    (a) no bar   E

    (b) 1 or 2 bars F

44. <u>MEDAL FOR SOUTH AFRICA CAMPAIGN 1834–53</u> (1854)

Issued for the campaigns of 1834–5, 1846–7, 1850–3
and dated 1853. Obv. diademed head of Queen Victoria;
rev. British lion behind a bush with the legend
<u>SOUTH AFRICA</u> and the date <u>1853</u>. Ribbon: yellow with
blue stripes   E

45. <u>INDIA GENERAL SERVICE MEDAL 1854</u> (Illustration No.
23)

Only issued with a bar, to cover a large number of
minor wars and expeditions. Obv. effigy of Queen
Victoria; rev. figure of Winged Victory crowning a
seating warrior.

(a)	PEGU	D
(b)	PERSIA	D
(c)	NORTH–WEST FRONTIER	D
(d)	UMBEYLA	D
(e)	BHOOTAN	D
(f)	LOOSHAI	D
(g)	PERAK	D
(h)	JOWAKI 1877–8	D
(i)	NAGA 1879–80	F
(j)	BURMA 1885–7	
	(i) silver	D
	(ii) bronze	D
(k)	SIKKIM 1888	
	(i) silver	E
	(ii) bronze	E

(l) HAZARA 1888
        (i) silver   D
        (ii) bronze   D

(m) BURMA 1887-9
        (i) silver   D
        (ii) bronze   D

(n) CHIN LUSHAI 1889-90
        (i) silver   D
        (ii) bronze   D

(o) LUSHAI 1889-92
        (i) silver   E
        (ii) bronze   E

(p) SAMANA 1891
        (i) silver   D
        (ii) bronze   D

(q) HAZARA 1891
        (i) silver   D
        (ii) bronze   D

(r) N.E. FRONTIER 1891
        (i) silver   D
        (ii) bronze   D

(s) HUNZA 1891
        (i) silver   F
        (ii) bronze   F

(t) BURMA 1889-92
        (i) silver   D
        (ii) bronze   D

(u) CHIN HILLS 1892-3
        (i) silver   G
        (ii) bronze   F

(v) KACHIN HILLS 1892-3
        (i) silver   H
        (ii) bronze   G

(w) WAZIRISTAN 1894-5
        (i) silver   D
        (ii) bronze   D

Medals to Indian recipients are at the lower end of
the price bracket and to British ones at the higher
end. The price of multiple-bar medals varies greatly

according to the combination of bars and the unit,
in the case of the more common multiple bars they
are worth approximately the same as the highest-
priced single bar amongst them.

46. CRIMEA MEDAL 1854-6 (Illustration No. 21)

The following bars were issued: ALMA, INKERMANN,
AZOFF, BALAKLAVA SEBASTOPOL. The maximum to any
recipient was four. The medals were issued to French
troops who took part in the operations, and they can
be found with the unofficial bars: KINNBURN, MALAKOF,
MER D'AZOFF and TRATKIR - as well as the above-
mentioned official ones.

		Unnamed	Engraved	Impressed
(a)	no bar	D	D	D
(b)	1 bar	D	D	D
(c)	2 bars	D	E	F
(d)	3 bars	E	F	F
(e)	4 bars	F	F	F

This medal, with the BALAKLAVA bar, is worth
considerably more when issued to the following units
who saw action on 25 October 1954:

(f)	93rd Foot	-	G	H
(g)	Heavy Brigade	-	G	H
(h)	Light Brigade	-	I	J

Obv. effigy of Queen Victoria and the date 1854;
rev. flying figure of Victory crowning a Roman
warrior. Ribbon: blue with yellow edging.

47. BALTIC MEDAL 1854-5

Obv. effigy of Queen Victoria; rev. Britannia seated
holding a trident with the legend BALTIC, 1854-1856.
Essentially a naval medal, but issued to a small
party of sappers and miners as well. Issued unnamed,
but named privately in some cases. Ribbon: yellow
with blue edges.

(a)   unnamed   D

(b)   name engraved   D

(c)   name impressed   D

(d)   name impressed to sappers and miners   I

48.   INDIAN MUTINY 1857-8

Obv. Queen Victoria's effigy; rev. Britannia and lion
with the legend INDIA and dates 1857-1858. Ribbon:
white with two red stripes. Five bars were issued,
with a maximum of four to any recipient. The bars
were DELHI, RELIEF OF LUCKNOW, LUCKNOW, CENTRAL INDIA.

(a)   no bar   D

(b)   1 bar   E

(c)   2 bars   F

(d)   3 bars   H

(e)   4 bars   I

The bar DEFENCE OF LUCKNOW, in combination with
others is valued at:

(f)   for members of the original defending
      force   G

(g)   for members of the first relief force   G

It is more valuable when issued without other bars.

49.   CHINA MEDAL 1857-60

Same medal as No. 40, but without the date 1842. The
following bars were issued: CHINA 1842, FATSHAN 1857,
CANTON 1857, TAKU FORTS 1858, TAKU FORTS 1860,
PEKIN 1860.

	Named	Unnamed (to the navy)
(a) no bar	D	D
(b) 1 bar	D	D
(c) 2 bars	E	D

(d)	3 bars	F	E
(e)	4 bars	G	F
(f)	5 bars	no recent valuation	

The bar CHINA 1842 is rare and therefore not included
in the above valuation.

50. NEW ZEALAND - SECOND WAR 1860-6 (1869)

Same design as No. 42, but with different dates.

1860	J
1860-1	F
1860-3	I
1860-4	E
1860-5	E
1860-6	F
1861	no recent valuation
1861-3	no recent valuation
1861-4	G
1861-5	no recent valuation
1861-6	E
1862-6	J
1863	no recent valuation
1863-4	F
1863-5	F
1863-6	F
1864	F
1864-5	F
1864-6	E
1865	G
1865-6	F
1866	F

51. CANADA GENERAL SERVICE MEDAL 1866-70 (1899)

Obv. Queen Victoria, with crown and veil and the
legend VICTORIA REGINA ET IMPERATRIX; rev. Canadian
flag surrounded by a maple wreath, above the legend
CANADA. The following bars were issued:

(a)	FENIAN RAID 1866	F
(b)	FENIAN RAID 1870	F

                (c) RED RIVER 1870   I

                (a) and (b) two bars   F

52. ABYSSINIA MEDAL 1867-8

     Obv. small bust of Queen Victoria in the centre of a
     nine-pointed star, between the points of which the
     letters forming ABYSSINIA. The medal is in silver
     and circular; rev. laurel wreath inside which is the
     name, rank and unit of the recipient. Ribbon: red
     with two white stripes on the edges.

          (a) British recipients, name etc die-struck F

          (b) Indian recipients, name etc impressed
               or engraved   D

53. ASHANTI MEDAL 1873-4

     Obv. effigy of Queen Victoria; rev. scenes of
     fighting between British forces and natives.

          (a) no bar   E

          (b) COOMASSIE   F

54. MEDAL FOR SOUTH AFRICA 1877-9

     Same design as No. 44.

          (a) no bar   D   (e) 1878   E
          (b) 1877   I   (f) 1878-79   E
          (c) 1877-78   E   (g) 1879   E
          (d) 1877-8-9   E

     Medals to recipients who took part in the actions at
     Rorkes Drift and Isandhlwana are worth much more.

55. MEDAL FOR AFGHANISTAN 1878-80

     Obv. Queen Victoria with diadem and veil, legend
     VICTORIA REGINA ET IMPERATRIX; rev. column of British
     troops on the march with native cavalry, officer on
     horseback and elephant carrying a machine gun.

Legend AFGHANISTAN 1878-79-80. Six bars were issued:
ALI MUSJID, PEIWAR KOTAL, CHARASIA, KABUL, AHMED KHEL,
KANDAHAR. Maximum to any one recipient: four.
Ribbon: crimson and green.

(a)	no bar	C
(b)	1 bar	D
(c)	2 bars	E
(d)	3 bars	F
(e)	4 bars	G

56. KABUL TO KANDAHAR STAR (1880)

Bronze five-pointed star with radiations. Obv. cipher
V.R.I. and the legend KABUL TO KANDAHAR and date 1880;
rev. plain, with the name, rank and regiment of the
recipient. Ribbon: red, yellow and blue, colours
merging into each other.

(a)	unnamed	D
(b)	British troops, impressed name	E
(c)	Indian troops, engraved name	D

57. CAPE OF GOOD HOPE GENERAL SERVICE MEDAL 1880-97

Obv. effigy of Queen Victoria with legend VICTORIA
REGINA ET IMPERATRIX; rev. the arms of the Cape
Colony with the legend CAPE OF GOOD HOPE. Ribbon:
blue with purple central stripe.

(a)	TRANSKEI	G
(b)	BASUTOLAND	G
(c)	BECHUANALAND	F
(d)	2 bars	G
(e)	3 bars	K

58. EGYPTIAN MEDAL 1882-9 (Illustration No. 24)

Obv. effigy of Queen Victoria with legend VICTORIA
REGINA ET IMPERATRIX; rev. Sphinx on a pedestal with

the legend EGYPT. Ribbon: blue and white vertical
stripes.

(a)	no bar, reverse dated 1882	E
(b)	no bar, no date	E
(c)	ALEXANDRIA 11th JULY	D
(d)	TEL-EL-KEBIR	D
(e)	EL-TEB	D
(f)	TAMAII	E
(g)	EL-TEB-TAMAII	D
(h)	SUAKIN 1884	D
(i)	THE NILE 1884-85	D
(j)	SUAKIN 1885	D
(k)	GEMAIZAH	D
(l)	TOSKI 1889	E

ABU KLEA, KIRBEKAN and TOFREK were not issued
as single bars

(m)	2 bars	D
(n)	3 bars	E
(o)	4 bars	F
(p)	5 bars	G

59. KHEDIVE BRONZE EGYPT STARS 1882-91

Obv. five-pointed bronze star in the centre of which
is a view of the Sphinx, the Pyramids and the desert
surrounded by the legend EGYPT 1882 and, in Arabic,
KHEDIVE OF EGYPT 1299. The Khedive's monogram and a
crown on the rev. Ribbon: plain blue

(a)	undated	B
(b)	undated with TOKAR clasp	D
(c)	dated 1882	B
(d)	dated 1884-86	C
(e)	dated 1884	C

60. NORTH-WEST CANADA MEDAL 1885

Obv. effigy of Queen Victoria with legend VICTORIA
REGINA ET IMPERATRIX; rev. legend NORTH WEST CANADA
and the date 1885 within a maple wreath. Ribbon:
blue with two crimson stripes.

		No bar	SASKATCHEWAN
(a)	unnamed	E	F
(b)	named	F	H

61. EAST AND WEST AFRICA MEDAL 1887-1900

Same design as No. 53. All medals were issued with a
bar, except in the case of (a) on which the name and
date are shown on the rim of the medal.

(a)	M'WELE 1895-6	D
(b)	1887-8	E
(c)	WITU 1890	D
(d)	1891-92	F
(e)	1892	E
(f)	WITU AUGUST 1893	F
(g)	LIWONDI 1893	I
(h)	JUBA RIVER 1893	I
(i)	LAKE NYASSA 1893	I
(j)	1893-94	F
(k)	GAMBIA 1894	E
(l)	BENIN RIVER 1894	E
(m)	BRASS RIVER 1895	E
(n)	1896-97	K
(o)	1896-98	F
(p)	NIGER 1897	I
(q)	BENIN 1897	E
(r)	DAWKITA 1897	J

(s)	1897-98	E
(t)	1898	F
(u)	SIERRA-LEONE 1896-99	E
(v)	1899	G
(w)	1900	F

In the case of medals with two bars, add 10 per cent
to the price of the highest valued bar; for medals
with three bars, add 25 per cent and for medals with
four bars add 50 per cent.

62. BRITISH SOUTH AFRICA COMPANY MEDAL 1893-7

Obv. effigy of Queen Victoria with the legend
VICTORIA REGINA; rev. lion charging over native
weapons with legend BRITISH SOUTH AFRICA COMPANY and
the name and date of the action. Ribbon: yellow with
three blue vertical stripes.

(a)	rev. MATABELAND 1893	F
(b)	do., RHODESIA 1896	G
(c)	do., MASHONALAND 1897	G
(d)	do., RHODESIA 1896 with 1 bar	F
(e)	no name or date on rev. with bar MASHONALAND 1890 (issued 1926)	I

63. CENTRAL AFRICA MEDAL 1891-8

Same medal as No. 53, but with different ribbon:
black, white and brown.

    (a)   first medal approved 1895 for campaigns
between 1891 and 1894. No bar, ring
suspension   F

    (b)   second medal approved 1899 for campaigns
between 1894 and 1898, with plain silver-
clasp suspension, and bar CENTRAL AFRICA
1894-98   I

64. <u>JUMMOO AND KASHMIR MEDAL 1895</u>

Bronze kidney-shaped medal, issued to native troops
only. Obv. coat of arms with two native soldiers,
native inscription and the names <u>JUMMOO AND KASHMIR</u>;
rev. fortress with troops in the foreground. With
bar <u>CHITRAL 1895</u>   F

65. <u>INDIA GENERAL SERVICE MEDAL 1895-1902</u>

Obv. effigy of Queen Victoria, except that the last
of the series has Edward VII's head; rev. British
and Indian soldier holding a flag with <u>INDIA 1895</u>.

		Silver	Bronze
(a)	DEFENCE OF CHITRAL 1895	H	G
(b)	RELIEF OF CHITRAL	C	D
(c)	PUNJAB FRONTIER 1897/98	D	D
(d)	MALAKAND 1897	E	D
(e)	SAMANA 1897	D	D
(f)	TIRAH 1897-98	D	D
(g)	WAZIRISTAN 1901-02	D	D

Multiple-bar medals, excluding the bars (a) and
(d):

		Silver	Bronze
(h)	2 bars	D	D
(i)	3 bars	D	D
(j)	4 bars	E	E

66. <u>ASHANTI STAR 1896</u>

Obv. four-pointed bronze star with St Andrew's cross
in between, a crown in the centre and the legend
ASHANTI 1896; rev. plain, with the legend <u>FROM THE</u>
<u>QUEEN</u>. Ribbon: yellow with two black vertical stripes.
Unnamed   E

67. <u>QUEEN'S SUDAN MEDAL 1896-7</u>

Obv. half-length effigy of Queen Victoria with
legend <u>VICTORIA REGINA ET IMPERATRIX</u>; rev. seated

Victory and a trophy of draped flags with the legend
SUDAN below. Ribbon: black and yellow with scarlet
stripe.

		Silver	Bronze
(a)	named	E	F
(b)	unnamed	D	E

68. KHEDIVE'S SUDAN MEDAL 1896-1908

Obv. oval shield with stars and crescents and a
trophy of flags and arms; rev. Turkish inscription.

(a)	silver, no bar, unnamed	D
(b)	do., named	D
(c)	bronze, no bar, unnamed	E
(d)	FIRKET	D
(e)	HAFIR	D
(f)	ABU HAMED	D
(g)	SUDAN 1897	D
(h)	THE ATBARA	F
(i)	KHARTOUM	D
(j)	GEDAREF	D
(k)	GEDID	D
(l)	BAHR-EL-GHAZEL 1900-02	E
(m)	JEROK	E
(n)	NYAM-NYAM	E
(o)	TALODI	F
(p)	KATFIA	F
(q)	NYIMA	F

Unnamed medals with multiple bars:

(r)	2 bars	D
(s)	3 bars	D
(t)	4 bars	E

(u)	5 bars	F
(v)	6 bars	G
(w)	7 bars	G

69. <u>BRITISH NORTH BORNEO COMPANY'S MEDALS 1897-1937</u>

Obv. the arms of the company supported by two native
figures with the motto PERGO ET PERAGO; rev. British
lion standing in front of a flag, with the legend
BRITISH NORTH BORNEO, also the name of the makers
SPINK & SON, LONDON.

		Silver	Bronze
(a)	punitive expedition medal, no bar	G	E
(b)	do., PUNITIVE EXPEDITION	G	E
(c)	medal, dated 1900, TAMBUNAN	G	D
(d)	do., RUNDUM	G	not issued
(e)	general-service medal without bar	F	-

The bronze medals were issued to natives and
exchanged for silver ones in 1906. The medal changed
its obv. and (c), (d) and (e) are different from (a)
and (b); there were also some changes in the rev.,
but they are all clearly marked BRITISH NORTH BORNEO.
The medals are often offered unnamed without the S
of SPINK or SON; they are specimen and worth about
half the price of the original. The ribbon also
underwent changes from, originally, watered orange
to yellow with a central green strip and, for (e),
to green and orange.

70. <u>EAST AND CENTRAL AFRICA MEDAL 1897-9</u>

Same obv. as for No. 67; rev. standing Britannia
with trident in one hand and a scroll and palm in
the other, legend EAST AND CENTRAL AFRICA. Always
issued with a bar. Ribbon: yellow and red.

| (a) | LUBWA'S (not issued singly) | G |

(b) UGANDA 1897-98   G

(c) 1898   G

(d) UGANDA 1899   G

71. QUEEN'S SOUTH AFRICA MEDAL 1899-1902 (Illustration
     No. 25)

Obv. effigy of Queen Victoria with veil and crown,
legend VICTORIA REGINA ET IMPERATRIX; rev. standing
Britannia with a flag and laurel wreath in her hand.
There are three types:

    (i)   with the wreath pointing to the letter
          F of AFRICA

    (ii) with the wreath pointing to the letter
          R of AFRICA

    (iii) with dates 1899-1900 (later removed from
          the die).

These are very rare and issued mainly to Lord
Strathcona's Horse. The prices indicated are for
obv. (i) or (ii); sometimes the dates can be seen
but not in relief as for rev. (iii). Ribbon: red,
blue and orange vertical stripes.

    (a) without bar
         (i) silver   C
         (ii) bronze   E

    (b) CAPE COLONY   C

    (c) RHODESIA   E

    (d) RELIEF OF MAFEKING F

    (e) DEFENCE OF KIMBERLEY E

    (f) TALANA   E

    (g) ELANDSLAAGTE   E

    (h) DEFENCE OF LADYSMITH D

    (i) BELMONT   D

    (j) MODDER RIVER   C

    (k) TUGELA HEIGHTS   C

(l)   NATAL   D

(m)   RELIEF OF KIMBERLEY   D

(n)   PAARDEBERG   D

(o)   ORANGE FREE STATE   C

(p)   RELIEF OF LADYSMITH   C

(r)   DRIEFONTEIN   C

(s)   WEPENER   G

(t)   DEFENCE OF MAFEKING   I

(u)   TRANSVAAL   C

(v)   JOHANNESBURG   C

(w)   LAING'S NECK   C

(x)   DIAMOND HILL   C

(y)   WITTEBERGEN   D

(z)   BELFAST   C

(yy) SOUTH AFRICA 1901   C

(zz) SOUTH AFRICA 1902   C

Some bars are rarer as a single bar. Prices for
multiple bars are:

(i)   2 bars, 3 bars, 4 bars, 5 bars C

(ii) 6 bars, 7 bars   D

(iii) 8 bars   E

72. QUEEN'S MEDITERRANEAN MEDAL 1899-1902

Same medal as above with same ribbon, but legend
MEDITERRANEAN instead of SOUTH AFRICA   E

73. TRANSPORT MEDAL 1899-1902

Obv. Edward VII in naval uniform; rev. map with
vessel and the legend OB PATRIAM MILITIBUS PER MARE
TRANSVECTI ADJUTAM. Ribbon: red with two blue stripes.

(a)   SOUTH AFRICA 1899-1902   F

(b) CHINA 1900   G

(c) with both bars   H

74. ASHANTI MEDAL (1901)

Obv. effigy of Edward VII; rev. British lion looking towards the sun. Legend ASHANTI. Ribbon: green with three black vertical stripes.

    (a) no bar
          (i) silver   F
          (ii) bronze   F

    (b) KUMASSI
          (i) silver   F
          (ii) bronze   G

75. CHINA MEDAL (1900) (1902)

Obv. effigy of Queen Victoria; rev. same as the China Medal of 1842 with new date 1900. Ribbon: crimson with yellow edges.

		Silver	Bronze
(a)	no bar	D	D
(b)	TAKU FORTS	D	–
(c)	DEFENCE OF LEGATIONS	J	–
(d)	RELIEF OF PEKIN	E	E
(e)	two bars – excluding (c)	F	F

76. KING EDWARD'S SOUTH AFRICAN MEDAL (1901-02)

Obv. effigy of Edward VII; rev. as for No. 71. Ribbon: green, white and orange.

    (a) without bars   D

    (b) with two bars SOUTH AFRICA 1901 and
         SOUTH AFRICA 1902   C

Very few were awarded with only one bar, and these need to be verified.

77.   <u>AFRICA GENERAL SERVICE MEDAL 1902</u>

Not awarded without a bar. The first thirty-four bars
bear the effigy of Edward VII; the ten following ones
(1913–20) bear the effigy of George V, and, after a
lapse of thirty-five years, it was issued again in
1955 with Queen Elizabeth II's effigy for the Kenya
campaign. Rev. as for No. 70 but with the legend
<u>AFRICA</u> only. Ribbon: yellow with green stripes.

      (a)   Edward VIII medals   E (a few F)

      (b)   George V medals   F (with <u>SHIMBER BERRIS</u>
                                            <u>1914/15</u> bar   H)

      (c)   Elizabeth II with bar
              <u>KENYA</u>   D

Medals awarded to British troops are usually in the
upper part of the bracket and to native troops in
the lower. Some medals were awarded in bronze, either
without a bar D or on a few occasions with a
bar E. Valuation of medals with multiple bars vary
very much according to the bars, unit, whether the
holder was British or native, etc.

78.   <u>TIBET MEDAL 1903–4</u>

Obv. effigy of Edward VII; rev. view of Lhasa with
legend TIBET 1903–4. Ribbon: green and white stripes
with a central purple one.

		Bronze	Silver
(a)	no bar	D	D
(b)	<u>GYANTSE</u>	E	E

The above valuations are for medals to native troops;
those issued to British are much more valuable.

79.   <u>MEDAL FOR THE NATAL ZULU RISING 1906</u>

Obv. effigy of Edward VII; rev. figure of Natal
supported by Britannia with natives in the background.
Legend <u>NATAL</u>.

(a) without bar   F

(b) with bar 1906   F

80. <u>INDIA GENERAL SERVICE MEDAL 1908-35</u>

Obv.

(i)   Edward VII, military bust with legend
      <u>EDWARDUS VII KAISAR-I-HIND</u>

(ii) George V, crowned bust, legend <u>GEORGIUS
      KAISAR-I-HIND</u> (Illustration No. 36)

(iii) same, but with legend <u>GEORGIUS V.D.G.
      BRITT : OMN : REX : ET. INDIAE. IMP</u>
      (Illustration No. 37).

Rev. fort at Khyber Pass, legend <u>INDIA</u>. This medal
is always issued with a bar. Only (a) and (b)
were issued in silver and bronze; all medals were
silver afterwards. Ribbon: green with central blue
stripe.

(a) <u>NORTH WEST FRONTIER 1908</u>

     (i) bronze   C
     (ii) silver   C

(b) <u>ABOR 1911-12</u>

     (i) as a second bar on Edward VII medal,
         either silver or bronze   G
     (ii) on George V bronze medal; obv.
          (ii)   F
    (iii) do., silver   F

(c) <u>AFGHANISTAN N.W.F.1919</u>; obv. (ii)   B

(d) <u>WAZIRISTAN 1919-21</u>; do.   B

(e) <u>MAHSUD</u> (always with previous bar);
     <u>obv.</u> (ii)   D

(f) <u>MALABAR 1921-22</u>; obv. (ii)   D

(g) <u>WAZIRISTAN 1921-24</u>; do.   C

(h) <u>WAZIRISTAN 1925</u>; do.   I
                              (only issued to RAF)

(i) <u>NORTH WEST FRONTIER 1930-31</u>; obv.
     (iii)   C

(j) <u>BURMA 1930-32</u>; obv. (iii)   C

(k) <u>MOHMAND 1933</u>; do.   D

(1) <u>NORTH WEST FRONTIER 1935</u>; do.   C

The above valuations are for medals to Indian troops,
except (h). Medals for British troops are worth
about 25 per cent more and, for the RAF, at least
double the indicated valuations.

81. <u>KHEDIVE SUDAN MEDAL 1910-18</u> (1911)

Obv. cipher of the khedive Abbas Hilmi and the date.
In 1918 this medal was modified to bear the cipher
of the new sultan, Hussein Kamil; rev. lion standing,
with the desert, trees and sky behind; underneath a
tablet with the word <u>SUDAN</u>. Issued unnamed. Bronze
medals without bars; <u>silver</u> both with and without
bars. Ribbon: green and red vertical stripes.

(a) bronze medal, 1st Khedive cipher,
     no bar   F

(b) do., 2nd cipher   F

(c) silver medal, 1st Khedive cipher,
     no bar   D

(d) do., 2nd cipher   E

(e) ATWOT   E

(f) S. KORDOFAN 1910   E

(g) SUDAN 1912   E

(h) ZERAF 1913-14   F

(i) MANDAL   F

(j) MIRI   F

(k) MONGALLA 1915-16   F

(1) DARFUR 1916   E

(m) FASHER   E

(n) LAU NUER   E

(o) NYIMA 1917-18   D

(p) ATWOT 1918   E

(q)	GARJAK NUER	E
(r)	ALIAB DINKA	G
(s)	NYALA	F
(t)	DARFUR 1921	F
(u)	DARFUR 1924	F

82. <u>1914 STAR</u> (1917)

Obv. star-shaped bronze medal with crossed swords,
laurel wreath, surmounted by the imperial crown and
with the dates <u>AUG – 1914 – NOV</u>; rev. plain, with
number, rank and regiment of the recipient. This
medal is also issued with the bar <u>5TH AUG – 22ND
NOV 1914</u>. Ribbon: red, white and blue.

 (a) without bar C

 (b) with bar   C

83. <u>1914–15 STAR</u> (1918)

Same as for the previous medal, but with the date
altered to 1914–15 B

84. <u>BRITISH WAR MEDAL 1914–20</u> (1919) (Illustration No.
39)

Obv. effigy of George V; rev. St George on horseback
with the dates 1914–1918. Ribbon: orange centre
stripe with narrow blue, black and white stripes.

 (a) silver   A

 (b) bronze (much harder to find) C

85. <u>VICTORY MEDAL 1914–18</u> (Illustration No. 40)

Obv. winged figure of Victory; rev. legend <u>THE GREAT
WAR FOR CIVILISATION</u> and dates 1914–1919. Ribbon:
wide watered ribbon with red in the centre shading
towards the edges to yellow, green, blue and
violet A

The same medal was issued to the South African forces

41   obv. GREAT BRITAIN, 1939–45 Star

42   obv. GREAT BRITAIN, France and Germany Star

43   obv. GREAT BRITAIN, Defence Medal

44   obv. GREAT BRITAIN, War Medal 1939–45

45   obv. GREAT BRITAIN, Korean War Medal

46   obv. UNITED NATIONS, Korea Medal

47   obv. GREAT BRITAIN, General Service Medal 1962, bar
'BORNEO'

48   obv. GREAT BRITAIN, Order of the British Empire, Member's
badge, civil division

49   obv. GREAT BRITAIN, Imperial Service Medal, King George
VI issue

50   obv. GREAT BRITAIN, Indian General Service Medal
1936–9, with bar 'NORTH WEST FRONTIER 1936–37',
Calcutta Mint issue

51   rev. GREAT BRITAIN, Colonial Police Long Service Medal
(note the brooch issued with the medal)

52   obv. GREAT BRITAIN, Special Constabulary Medal 1918 with
bar. 'The Great War 1914–18', King George V issue

49 is used to illustrate a type of obv. only, and is not described

53 obv. GREAT BRITAIN, King George VI Coronation Medal
1937 (issued to a lady)

54 obv. GREAT BRITAIN, Queen Elizabeth II Coronation Medal
1953

55 obv. GREAT BRITAIN, Naval Long Service and Good
Conduct Medal, King George VI issue, coinage head,
1st type 1937–48

56 obv. GREAT BRITAIN, General Service Medal (Army and
RAF) 1918–62 Queen Elizabeth, 2nd issue, with bar
'ARABIAN PENINSULA'

57 obv. GREAT BRITAIN, Air Crew Europe Star

58 obv. GREAT BRITAIN, Africa Star, with bar '8th ARMY'

59 obv. GREAT BRITAIN, Atlantic Star, with bar 'FRANCE
AND GERMANY'

60 obv. GREAT BRITAIN, General Service Medal (Army and
RAF) 1918–62 King George VI issue, 1st type obv., with
bar 'S.E. ASIA 1945–46'

61 obv. GREAT BRITAIN, do., King George VI, 2nd type obv.,
without 'INDIAE IMP, bar 'PALESTINE 1945–48'

with the legend in English and Afrikaans THE GREAT
WAR FOR CIVILISATION - DE GROTE OORLOG VOOR DE
BESCHAVING - 1914-1919   C

Mentions in despatches were indicated by a bronze
leaf worn on the ribbon of this medal. Unless the
mention is verified, this does not affect the value;
if it is verified   B

86. MERCANTILE MARINE WAR MEDAL 1914-18 (1919)

Obv. effigy of George V; rev. a merchant vessel
amongst the waves with a submarine and a sailing
vessel in the background. Ribbon: red and green with
a white central stripe   B

87. TERRITORIAL WAR MEDAL 1914-19 (1920)

Obv. effigy of George V; rev. legend TERRITORIAL
WAR MEDAL, VOLUNTARY SERVICE OVERSEAS 1914-1919.
Ribbon: yellow with two green stripes   C

88. NAVAL GENERAL SERVICE MEDAL 1915-62

Obv. effigy of the reigning sovereign; rev.
Britannia and sea horses. This medal was never issued
without a bar. Ribbon: crimson with three white
stripes.

(a) George V, naval bust

        (i) PERSIAN GULF 1909-14   D
       (ii) IRAQ 1919-20   I
      (iii) N.W. PERSIA 1920   J

(b) George VI, crowned head

Legend GEORGIUS VI D : G : BR : OMN : REX ET INDIAE
IMP.

       (iv) PALESTINE 1936-1939   D
        (v) S.E. ASIA 1945-46   C
       (vi) PALESTINE 1945-48   C
      (vii) MALAYA   C

(c) George VI, crowned head

Legend GEORGIUS VI DEI : GRA : BRITT : OMN: REX :
F.D.DEF.

    (viii) MALAYA   C

    (ix) YANGTZE (when awarded to the crew of
HMS Amethyst, worth double)   G

    (x) MINESWEEPING 1945–51   F

(d) Elizabeth II, crowned head

Legend ELIZABETH II D : G : BR : OMN : REGINA F.D.

    (xi) MALAYA   C

    (xii) BOMB AND MINE CLEARANCE 1945–53   H

(e) Elizabeth II, crowned head

Legend ELIZABETH II DEI GRATIA REGINA F.D.

    (xiii) MALAYA   C

    (xiv) BOMB AND MINE CLEARANCE 1945–53   H

    (xv) BOMB AND MINE CLEARANCE,
MEDITERRANEAN   I

    (xvi) CYPRUS   D

    (xvii) NEAR EAST   D

    (xviii) ARABIAN PENINSULA   E

    (xix) BRUNEI   E

89. GENERAL SERVICE MEDAL (ARMY AND RAF) 1918–62

Obv. effigy of the reigning sovereign; rev. winged
figure of Victory. Ribbon: purple, green, purple.

(a) George V, coinage head

    (i) S. PERSIA   D

    (ii) KURDISTAN   C

    (iii) IRAQ   C

    (iv) N.W. PERSIA   C

    (v) SOUTHERN DESERT : IRAQ (RAF only)   H

(b) George V, crowned bust

       (vi) N. KURDISTAN (RAF only)   J

(c) George VI, crowned head

Legend GEORGIUS VI D : G : BR : OMN : REX ET INDIAE IMP.

      (vii)   PALESTINE (Illustration No. 60)   C
      (viii) S.E. ASIA 1945-46 (i) unnamed B
                              (ii) named   C
       (ix)   BOMB AND MINE CLEARANCE 1945-49 G
        (x)   PALESTINE 1945-48 (Illustration No. 61)   C
       (xi)   MALAYA   C

(d) George VI, crowned head

Legend GEORGIUS VI DEI GRA : BRIT : OMN : REX : FID : DEF.

      (xii)   BOMB AND MINE CLEARANCE 1945-49 G
      (xiii) PALESTINE 1945-48   C
      (xiv) MALAYA   C

(e) Elizabeth II, crowned head

Legend ELIZABETH II D.G. : BR : OMN : REGINA F.D.

      (xv)   MALAYA   C

(f) Elizabeth II, crowned head

Legend ELIZABETH II DEI GRATIA REGINA F.D.

      (xvi)   MALAYA   C
      (xvii) CYPRUS   C
      (xviii) NEAR EAST   C
      (xix)   ARABIAN PENINSULA (Illustration No. 56)   D
      (xx)   BRUNEI   D
      (xxi)   BOMB AND MINE CLEARANCE 1945-56 G

90. <u>INDIAN GENERAL SERVICE MEDAL 1936-9</u> (Illustration
     No. 50)

     Obv. crowned head of George VI; rev. tiger with
     legend <u>INDIA</u>. Never issued without a bar. Ribbon:
     green, <u>red</u> and grey.

> (a) <u>NORTH WEST FRONTIER 1936-37</u>, Royal Mint
>   issue to British troops   C
>
> (b) <u>NORTH WEST FRONTIER 1936-37</u>, Calcutta
>   Mint issue to Indian troops   C
>
> (c) <u>NORTH WEST FRONTIER 1937-39</u>, Royal Mint
>   issue to British troops   C
>
> (d) <u>NORTH WEST FRONTIER 1937-39</u>, Calcutta
>   Mint issue to Indian troops   C
>
> (e) 2 bars to British troops   D
>
> (f) 2 bars to Indian troops   C

     Royal Mint medals to British troops are at the upper
     end of the valuation bracket and Calcutta Mint medals
     to Indian troops at the lower end.

91. <u>WORLD WAR II STARS 1939-45</u>

     Bronze stars with six points, royal cipher in the
     centre, surmounted by a crown, and inscribed with
     the name of the star. Obv. plain, unnamed. These
     stars were also issued to Commonwealth troops, and
     in some cases were issued with name, rank and number.
     These are worth a little more, depending on the star
     and the unit.

> (a) 1939-45 Star (Illustration No. 41)   A
>   with bar <u>BATTLE OF BRITAIN</u>
>   <u>if verified</u>   D
>   Ribbon: dark blue, red and light blue.
>
> (b) Atlantic Star   B
>   with bar (i) <u>AIR CREW EUROPE</u>
>   <u>if verified</u>   C
>   (ii) <u>FRANCE AND GERMANY</u>   B
>   (Illustration No. 59)
>   Ribbon: watered dark blue, white and sea
>   green.

(c) Air Crew Europe Star (Illustration
     No. 57)   D
     with bar (i) ATLANTIC if verified   D
               (ii) FRANCE AND GERMANY if
                    verified   D
     Ribbon: light blue with black edges and
     two yellow stripes.

(d) Africa Star   A
     with bar (i) NORTH AFRICA 1942–43   A
               (ii) EIGHTH ARMY (Illustration
                    No. 58)   A
               (iii) FIRST ARMY   A
     Ribbon: sand colour with narrow dark blue,
     red and light-blue stripes.

(e) Burma Star   B
     with bar PACIFIC if verified   B
     Ribbon: dark blue with red, blue and
     orange stripes.

(f) Pacific Star   B
     with bar BURMA if verified   B
     Ribbon: dark green with red edges,
     central yellow stripe and thin dark-
     blue and light-blue stripes.

(g) Italy Star   A
     Ribbon: red, white and green.

(h) France and Germany Star (Illustration
     No. 42)   B
     with bar ATLANTIC if verified   B
     Ribbon: blue, white and red.

When the price of a star with a verified bar is
indicated in the same bracket, it is in the upper
part of the bracket, being worth more than the star
without. Bars which are not verified do not increase
the value of a star.

92. DEFENCE MEDAL (Illustration No. 43)

Obv. effigy of George VI, coinage head; rev. royal
crown with an oak tree and the dates 1939–1945 and
the legend THE DEFENCE MEDAL. Ribbon: bright orange
with green edges and black stripes.

(i)   cupro-nickel issue, unnamed   A

(ii)   silver issue to Canadian troops,
       unnamed   B

(iii) do., to Australian troops, named B

93. <u>WAR MEDAL 1939-45</u> (Illustration No. 44)

Obv. effigy of George VI, crowned head; rev. lion
trampling on a dragon, dated 1939-1945. Ribbon: red
central stripe with white, blue and red stripes.

(i)   cupro-nickel issue, unnamed   A

(ii)   silver issue to Canadian troops,
       unnamed   B

(iii) do., to Australian troops, named   B

Mention in despatches was indicated by a bronze oak
leaf on the ribbon of this medal, but this does not
affect the value unless it is verified.

94. <u>KOREAN WAR MEDAL 1950-3</u> (Illustration No. 45)

Obv. laureated bust of Elizabeth II; rev. Hercules
killing Hydra, legend <u>KOREA</u>. Circular medal in cupro-
nickel, the silver issue of which is listed under
CANADA. Ribbon: yellow with two blue stripes   C

95. <u>GENERAL SERVICE MEDAL 1962</u>

Obv. crowned head of Elizabeth II; rev. legend <u>FOR
CAMPAIGN SERVICE</u>, surrounded by a wreath with a
crown above. Issued to all services, never without
a bar. Ribbon: purple with green edges.

(a) <u>BORNEO</u> (Illustration No. 47) C

(b) <u>RADFAN</u>   D

(c) <u>SOUTH ARABIA</u>   C

(d) <u>MALAY PENINSULA</u>   D

(e) <u>SOUTH VIETNAM</u>   I
     (issued to Australian troops only)

(f) <u>NORTHERN IRELAND</u>   D

        (g)   DHOFAR   F

        (h)   2 bars   D   (combination of the first

        (i)   3 bars   E   four and sixth bars only)

96.   QUEEN VICTORIA JUBILEE MEDALS

(a)   Jubilee Medal 1887

Obv. Victoria's bust with veil and crown; rev. IN
COMMEMORATION OF THE 50TH YEAR OF THE REIGN OF QUEEN
VICTORIA 21 JUNE 1887. Ribbon: light-blue and dark-
blue stripes.

        (i)   gold   I

        (ii)   silver   D

        (iii) bronze   C

(b)   Police Jubilee Medal 1887

Obv. Victoria's bust with veil and diadem; rev.
JUBILEE OF HER MAJESTY QUEEN VICTORIA inscribed
round the service to which it was issued and dated
1887. Ribbon: plain blue.

                                          Bronze

        (i)   Metropolitan Police   C

        (ii)   City of London Police   C

        (iii) Police Ambulance Service   D

(c)   Jubilee Medal 1887, with 1897 bar

        (i)   gold   I

        (ii)   silver   D

        (iii) bronze   C

(d)   Police Jubilee Medal 1887, with 1897 bar

                                          Bronze

        (i)   Metropolitan Police   C

        (ii)   City of London Police   C

        (iii) Police Ambulance Service   E

(e) Jubilee Medal 1897

Same as (a), but on rev. 60TH instead of 50TH and
20TH JUNE 1897 instead of 21ST JUNE 1887. There were
no gold medals.

    (i)   silver   C

   (ii)   bronze   C

(f) Police Jubilee Medal 1897

Same as (b), but with date 1897 instead of 1887.

		Bronze
(i)	Metropolitan Police	B
(ii)	City of London Police	C
(iii)	Police Ambulance Service	E
(iv)	London County Council Metropolitan Fire Brigade (Illustration No. 30)	F
(v)	St John's Ambulance Brigade	E

(g) Queen Victoria's Visit to Ireland 1900 Medal

Obv. half-length effigy of Queen Victoria holding a
sceptre; rev. allegory of Hibernia with Kingstown
Harbour in the background. Ribbon: plain blue,
suspended from brooch bar with a shamrock in the
centre. Circular medal in bronze   D

97. KING EDWARD VII CORONATION MEDALS (1902-3)

(a) Coronation Medal (Illustration No. 31)

Obv. conjoined busts of King Edward VII and Queen
Alexandra; rev. cipher ER VII, surmounted by a
crown with the date 26 JUNE 1902 underneath.
Ribbon: blue with central red stripe.

    (i)   silver   C

   (ii)   bronze   B

<u>(b) Police Coronation Medal</u>

Obv. Edward VII crowned in Coronation robes; rev.
<u>CORONATION OF HIS MAJESTY EDWARD VII 1902</u>. Crown and
laurel and oak branches underneath and the name of
the service round it. Ribbon: red with thin blue
stripe in the centre.

		<u>Bronze</u>
(i)	Metropolitan Police	D
(ii)	City of London Police	D
(iii)	LCC Metropolitan Fire Brigade	D
(iv)	St John's Ambulance Brigade	D
(v)	County and Borough Police	D
(vi)	Police Ambulance Service	D

(vii) Scottish Police 1903
       (Illustration No. 32).
       Same as above, but rev.
       legend reads <u>FROM HIS MAJESTY</u>
       <u>KING EDWARD VII</u> and date 1903;
       around the circumference
       <u>SCOTTISH POLICE</u>   D

(viii) Visit to Ireland 1903
       Obv. as for 97(b) above; rev.
       as for 96(g), with date 1903;
       pale blue ribbon   D

(ix)   Delhi Durbar Medal 1903
       Obv. King Edward VII effigy facing to the
       right instead of to the left; legend
       <u>EDWARD VII DELHI DARBAR 1903</u>; rev. legend
       in Persian meaning <u>BY THE GRACE OF THE</u>
       <u>LORD OF THE REALM EDWARD KING EMPEROR OF</u>
       <u>INDIA 1903</u>. Dia. 1½in; larger than usual.
       Ribbon: pale blue with three narrow dark-
       blue stripes.

          (i) gold   I

          (ii) silver D

98. <u>KING GEORGE V CORONATION AND JUBILEE MEDALS 1911-35</u>

(a) Coronation Medal 1911

Obv. conjointed busts of King George V and Queen Mary; rev. cipher GvR and date 22 June 1911, crown above. Ribbon: blue with two red central stripes. In silver only   C

(b) Police Coronation Medal 1911

Obv. King George V in Coronation robes, crowned; rev. crown in the centre surrounded by the name of the service and <u>CORONATION 1911</u>. Ribbon: red with three blue stripes. <u>In silver only.</u>

(i)	City of London Police	D
(ii)	Metropolitan Police	C
(iii)	County and Borough Police	C
(iv)	London Fire Brigade	D
(v)	Royal Irish Constabulary	D
(vi)	Scottish Police (Illustration No. 33)	D
(vii)	St Andrew Ambulance Corps	F
(viii)	St John's Ambulance Brigade	D
(ix)	Royal Parks	F
(x)	Police Ambulance Service	F
(xi)	Visit to Ireland	C

(xi) continued: Same obv., but reads <u>CORONATION 1911 - JULY 7-12</u>. Ribbon: green with two red stripes.

(xii) Delhi Durbar Medal 1911
Obv. conjointed busts of King George V and Queen Mary; rev. legend in Persian meaning <u>DURBAR OF GEORGE THE FIFTH EMPEROR OF INDIA AND KING AND LORD OF THE COUNTRIES OF THE ENGLISH</u>. Dia. 1½in; larger than usual. Same ribbon as the Coronation medal.

         (i) gold   H

         (ii) silver D

(xiii)   Silver Jubilee Medal 1935
          Obv. conjoined busts of King George V and
          Queen Mary with the legend GEORGE V AND
          QUEEN MARY MAY VI MCMXXV; rev. cipher GRI
          surmounted by a crown with the dates
          MAY 6 1910 and MAY 6 1935. Ribbon: red
          with white and blue stripes. Silver only
          C

99. KING GEORGE VI CORONATION MEDAL 1937 (Illustration
    No. 53)

    Obv. conjointed busts of King George VI and Queen
    Elizabeth, no legend; rev. royal cipher GRI
    surmounted by a crown, with the legend GEORGE VI
    QUEEN ELIZABETH — CROWNED 12 MAY 1937. Ribbon: blue
    with narrow red and white stripes   C

100. QUEEN ELIZABETH II CORONATION MEDAL 1953 (Illustration
     No. 54)

     Obv. bust of Queen Elizabeth II facing right, no
     legend; rev. royal cipher E ii R surmounted by
     crown, with legend QUEEN ELIZABETH II CROWNED 2nd
     JUNE 1953. Ribbon: red with two blue central
     stripes and white edges. Medals issued to ladies
     have the ribbon in the form of a bow. Issued in
     silver only   C

101. ARCTIC MEDAL 1818-55 (1857)

     Octagonal silver medal. Unnamed. Plain white ribbon.
     Obv. Queen Victoria's effigy; rev. ship in ice with
     icebergs. Legend FOR ARCTIC DISCOVERIES and dates
     1818-1855   F

102. ARCTIC MEDAL 1875-6 (1876)

     Round silver medal. Obv. effigy of Queen Victoria,
     with coronet and veil. Legend VICTORIA REGINA and
     date 1878; rev. sailing ship in ice, no legend.
     Plain white ribbon. Named   I

103. <u>POLAR MEDAL 1904</u>

Obv. effigy of the reigning sovereign; rev. sledge party in front of sailing vessel in ice. Octagonal medal with white ribbon. Named.

      (a) Edward VII, in admiral's uniform
            (i)   silver   J
            (ii) bronze   J

      (b) George V, in admiral's uniform
            (i)   silver   J
            (ii) bronze   J

      (c) George V, crowned in Coronation robes, bronze only   J

      (d) George V, coinage head, silver only   J

      (e) George VI, coinage head
            (i)   silver   J
            (ii) bronze   J

      (f) Elizabeth II, coinage head, legend <u>ELIZABETH II DEI GRA BRITT OMN REGINA F D</u>, silver only   J

      (g) do., with legend <u>ELIZABETH II DEI GRATIA REGINA F D</u>, silver only   J

Most of these medals have a clasp reading Antarctic or Arctic, followed by a date; these are not listed as there are more than 100 different ones, and whilst some are rarer than others, they are all within the indicated value range. The medals without clasps are bronze ones of Edward VII and George V type (b).

104. <u>NAVAL GOOD SHOOTING MEDAL 1903–14</u>

Obv. effigy of the reigning sovereign, Neptune with trident and legend <u>AMAT VICTORIA CURAM</u>. Plain silver circular medal. Ribbon: blue, white and red. Can be awarded with a bar giving name of ship, type of gun fired and the year.

      (a) Edward VII E
           with bar   G

        (b)   George V   F
              with bar   H

105. <u>ARMY BEST SHOT MEDAL</u> (MILITARY FORCES) (1869)

First issued as the Queen's Medal for champion shots
in the military forces, with the Queen's effigy on
the obv., and Fame standing on a dais on the rev.
Issued in bronze until 1872, then in silver until
1883 when it became obsolete. It was reinstituted in
1923 in silver as the King's Medal, with the King's
effigy and the same rev. It became again the Queen's
Medal in 1953, also in silver. A bar can be awarded
if it is won more than once. Ribbon: red wide central
stripe with white and black ones on the edges.

        (a)   Queen Victoria
                  (i)   silver   I
                  (ii) bronze   H

        (b)   King George V, silver   H

        (c)   King George VI, silver   I

        (d)   Queen Elizabeth, silver   I

106. <u>QUEEN'S MEDAL FOR CHAMPION SHOTS IN THE AIR FORCE</u> (1953)

Obv. effigy of Queen Elizabeth II; rev. Hermes
throwing a javelin, mounted on a hawk in flight.
Ribbon: very similar to King George V Silver Jubilee
Medal (1935). Clasp with the date worn on the ribbon.
More than one can be awarded if won in different
years   J

107. <u>MERITORIOUS SERVICE MEDAL</u> (1845)

Obv. effigy of the reigning sovereign; rev. <u>FOR
MERITORIOUS SERVICE</u> surrounded by a wreath. <u>Ribbon:
crimson until 1916</u> when white edges were added and
in 1917 a white centre stripe was further added.
During the period 1917-28, the MSM was awarded to
the Royal Navy with the King in admiral's uniform,
and to the RAF with coinage head.

(a)   Victoria young head (1845-1901)
          (i)   with date 1848 below bust   I
          (ii) no date   D

(b)   Edward VII, military bust (1902-10)   D

(c)   George V, military bust (1911-36)   C

(d)   do., coinage head (1930-6)   D

(e)   do., to RAF (1917-28)   E

(f)   George V, naval bust (1917-28) to
       Royal Navy   E

(g)   George VI, coinage head, legend
       GEORGIUS VI D.G.BR : OMN : REX F.D.
       IND:IMP: (1937-49)   C

(h)   do., without IND IMP (1949-52)   D

(i)   Elizabeth II, legend ELIZABETH II
       DEI GRA : BRITT : OMN : REGINA :
       F.D. (1952-3)   D

(j)   do., legend ELIZABETH II DEI GRATIA
       REGINA F.D. (since 1954)   D

108. AIR EFFICIENCY AWARD (1942)

Obv. effigy of the reigning sovereign; rev. AIR
EFFICIENCY AWARD. Silver. Ribbon: green with two
central pale-blue stripes.

(a)   George VI, legend GEORGIUS VI D.G. BR :
       OMN : REX ET INDIAE IMP (1942-9)   D

(b)   do., GEORGIUS VI DEI GRA : BRITT : OMN :
       REX FID : DEF (1949-52)   D

(c)   Elizabeth II, legend ELIZABETH II DEI
       GRA : BRITT : OMN : REGINA : F.D.
       (1952-3)   D

(d)   do., legend ELIZABETH II DEI GRATIA
       REGINA F.D. (since 1954)   D

109. NAVAL LONG SERVICE AND GOOD CONDUCT MEDAL (1831)

Obv. on (a) is crowned anchor; remainder, the effigy
of the reigning sovereign. Rev. on (a) gives

recipient's name, ship and length of service;
remainder a sailing ship with legend FOR LONG SERVICE
AND GOOD CONDUCT. Bars are awarded for further
service. Ribbon: blue with white edges.

(a)	1831-41	G
(b)	Victoria young head, 1848 below bust, wide suspender	I
(c)	do., no date (1841-74), wide suspender	D
(d)	do., but narrow suspender, $1\frac{1}{4}$in, name engraved	D
(e)	do., name impressed	C
(f)	Edward VII, naval bust (1902-10)	C
(g)	George V, naval bust (1911-24) (Illustration No. 34)	B
(h)	do., but fixed suspension (1924-8)	C
(i)	George V, coinage head (1928-36)	C
(j)	George VI, coinage head (1937-48) (Illustration No. 55)	C
(k)	do., without IND IMP (1949-52)	D
(l)	Elizabeth II, legend ELIZABETH II DEI : GRA : BRITT : OMN : REGINA : F : D (1952-3), fixed suspender	E
(m)	do., legend ELIZABETH II DEI GRATIA REGINA F.D., swivel suspender	C

110. <u>LONG SERVICE AND GOOD CONDUCT MEDAL (ARMY) 1830-1930</u>

Obv. military trophy of arms with those of William
IV and Hanover; rev. FOR LONG SERVICE AND GOOD
CONDUCT. Ribbon: crimson until 1916, when white
edges were added.

(a)	1830-1, small ring suspension	G
(b)	1831-7, do., but large ring or rectangular suspender, rim-dated	D
(c)	1837-55, William IV arms, excluding those of Hanover	D

(d) 1855-74, do., but silver-scroll suspender
     bar, large reverse letters   D

(e) 1874-1901, do., but small reverse
     letters   C

(f) 1901-11, Edward VII, military bust   C

(g) 1911-30, George V, military bust, swivel
     suspender   B

(h) do., fixed suspender (from 1924
     onwards)   C

111. <u>LONG SERVICE AND GOOD CONDUCT MEDAL</u> (MILITARY)
     (1930)

Same design as above, but a bar <u>REGULAR ARMY</u> is fixed
to the suspender. The same medal with the name of the
appropriate country instead of <u>REGULAR ARMY</u> was used
in the Commonwealth countries and is mentioned under
the appropriate countries. Same ribbon. Bars may be
added for further service.

(a) George V, military bust (1930-6)   C

(b) George VI, crowned head (1937-49)   C

(c) do., without IND IMP in legend
     (1949-52)   D

(d) Elizabeth II, crowned head, legend
     <u>ELIZABETH II DEI GR : BRITT : OMN :
     REGINA : F.D.</u> (1952-3)   D

(e) do., legend <u>ELIZABETH II DEI GRATIA
     REGINA F.D.</u> (since 1953)   C

112. <u>ROYAL AIR FORCE LONG SERVICE AND GOOD CONDUCT MEDAL</u>
     (1919)

Obv. effigy of the sovereign; rev. eagle in flight
with crown above, and the legend <u>FOR LONG SERVICE
AND GOOD CONDUCT</u>. Ribbon: central red and blue
stripes with narrow white stripes at the edges.

(a) George V, coinage head (1919-36)   D

(b) George VI, crowned (1937-49)   C

62 obv. CANADA, Canadian Volunteer Service Medal, 1939–45

63 rev. INDIA, India Service Medal, 1939–45

64 obv. IRELAND, General Service Medal 1917–21

65 obv. IRELAND, Emergency Service Medal 1939–46, with
bar

66 rev. do., without bar, issued to Defence Forces

67 obv. FEDERATION OF MALAYA, Federation of Malaya
Active Service Medal 1964

68 rev. NEW ZEALAND, New Zealand War Service Medal
1939–45

69 obv. PAKISTAN, Tamgha-i-Difa with bar 'KASHMIR 1948'

70 rev. PAKISTAN, Combined Forces Long Service Medal

71 obv. SOUTH AFRICA, Africa Service Medal 1939–45

72 obv. PORTUGAL, Medal for the Campaigns of 1826–34

73 obv. PORTUGAL, Good Conduct Medal, D. Luiz I issue, military bust without decorations

74 obv. PORTUGAL, Good Conduct Medal, D. Carlos I issue

75 obv. PORTUGAL, Mozambique Campaign Medal 1894–5

76 obv. PORTUGAL, Good Conduct Medal, Republican issue, 1910

77 obv. USA, National Defense Service Medal

78 obv. USA, Asiatic-Pacific Campaign Medal

79 obv. USA, Army Good Conduct Medal

80 obv. USA, American Defense Service Medal

81 obv. USA, European-African-Middle Eastern Campaign Medal

        (c) do., without <u>IND IMP</u> (1949-52)   D

        (d) Elizabeth II, crowned, legend
             <u>ELIZABETH II DEI GRA BRITT OMN</u>
             <u>REGINA F D</u> (1952-3)   D

        (e) do., legend <u>ELIZABETH DEI GRATIA</u>
             <u>REGINA F D</u> (since 1953)   C

113. <u>VOLUNTEER LONG SERVICE MEDAL</u> (1894-1930)
      (Illustration No. 26)

      Obv. effigy of the reigning sovereign; rev. laurel
      branches with legend <u>FOR LONG SERVICE IN THE</u>
      <u>VOLUNTEER FORCE</u>. Ribbon: plain green.

        (a) Victoria, with legend <u>VICTORIA REGINA</u>   B

        (b) do., with legend <u>VICTORIA REGINA AN</u>
             <u>ET IMPERATRIX</u> (issued to overseas
             auxiliary forces)   C

        (c) Edward VII, military bust, legend
             <u>EDWARDUS VII REX</u> (1902-8)   B

        (d) do., legend <u>EDWARDUS VII REX ET</u>
             <u>IMPERATOR</u> (for use in India)   C

        (e) do., legend <u>EDWARDUS VII KAISAR-I-</u>
             <u>HIND</u> (1902-10) (for use in India)   C

        (f) George V, military bust (1911-30)   C

114. <u>VOLUNTEER OFFICERS DECORATION</u> (1892-1908)

      Obv. oak wreath tied with ribbon round the royal
      cipher, a crown above; rev. plain with hallmark,
      sometimes the name of the holder. Ribbon: green.

        (a) VR (1892-1902)   C

        (b) VRI (do.)   D

        (c) ER VII (1902-8)   C

115. <u>TERRITORIAL DECORATION</u> (1908-1930)

      As above, but not hallmarked, and the ribbon has a
      yellow centre stripe.

(a) E vii R (1908-10)   C

(b) G v R (1911-30)   C

116. EFFICIENCY DECORATION (1930)

As above, but the medal is suspended from a bar
TERRITORIAL and, in the case of overseas units, the
name of the country in which the recipient served.
The ribbon remains the same, and bars can be awarded
for further service. Price brackets indicated are
for bar TERRITORIAL. Date of award on rev.

(a) G v R (1930-6)   C

(b) GRI (1937-48)   C

(c) G vi R (1948-52)   D

(d) ER II (since 1953) D

117. TERRITORIAL FORCE EFFICIENCY MEDAL (1908-30)

Oval medal. Obv. effigy of the reigning sovereign;
rev. (a) and (b) TERRITORIAL FORCE EFFICIENCY MEDAL,
(c) TERRITORIAL EFFICIENCY MEDAL. Ribbon: green with
yellow stripe.

(a) Edward VII, military bust (1908-10)   B

(b) George V, military bust (1911-20)   B
     (Illustration No. 35)

(c) do., modified rev. (1920-30)   B

118. EFFICIENCY MEDAL (1930)

Oval-shaped silver medal with obv. effigy of the
reigning sovereign; rev. FOR EFFICIENT SERVICE. The
medal is suspended from a bar attached to the fixed
suspender reading TERRITORIAL, MILITIA, ARMY
EMERGENCY RESERVE, or the name of the dominion or
crown colony where it was issued. The latter are
listed under the names of the country concerned.
Ribbon: green with yellow edges for TERRITORIAL,
dark blue with three yellow stripes for MILITIA and
ARMY EMERGENCY RESERVE.

    (a) George V, crowned bust (1930-6)

TERRITORIAL	B
MILITIA	C

    (b) George VI, crowned bust (1937-49)

TERRITORIAL	B
MILITIA	C

    (c) do., without INDIAE IMP (1949-52)

TERRITORIAL	C
MILITIA	D

    (d) Elizabeth II, legend ELIZABETH II DEI GRA BRITT OMN REGINA F D (1952-3)

TERRITORIAL	C
MILITIA	D
ARMY EMERGENCY RESERVE	D

    (e) do., legend ELIZABETH II DEI GRATIA REGINA F.D. (since 1953)

TERRITORIAL	C
ARMY EMERGENCY RESERVE	D

119. ARMY EMERGENCY RESERVE DECORATION (1951)

Same as No. 116, but with legend ARMY EMERGENCY RESERVE. Ribbon: dark blue with yellow central stripe.

    (a) G vi R (1951-2)   D

    (b) E II R (1953-)   C

120. ROYAL FLEET RESERVE LONG SERVICE AND GOOD CONDUCT MEDAL

Obv. effigy of the reigning sovereign; rev. a battleship with the legend DIUTURNE FIDELIS. Ribbon white with blue central stripe, brown stripes on each side, and white edges. The same medal is issued to the Royal Naval Reserve, Royal Naval Volunteer Reserve and Royal Naval Auxiliary Sick Berth Reserve. The only difference is in the ribbons, which are: for RNR, green until 1916, when a white central stripe and green edges were added; for RNVR

and RNASBR, dark blue with wide green central stripe
with red stripe on each side. The RNR and RNVR
merged in 1958. The medals are identified by the
edge naming, which includes the unit of the recipient.
The prices indicated are for the RFR, RNR and RNVR.
The RNASBR medals are worth much more and some of
them are quite rare.

  (a) Edward VII, naval bust (1908-10) B

  (b) George V, naval bust (1911-20) B

  (c) George V, coinage head (1920-36) B

  (d) George VI (1937-49) C

  (e) do., without IND IMP (1949-52) C

  (f) Elizabeth II, coinage head, legend
    ELIZABETH II DEI GRA BRITT OMN
    REGINA F D (1952-3) C

  (g) do., legend ELIZABETH II DEI GRATIA
    REGINA F D C

121. ROYAL NAVAL RESERVE DECORATION

Obv. oval-shaped medal, consisting of the royal
cipher surrounded by a cable tied into a reef knot
at the bottom, surmounted by a crown. Palin rev.,
hallmarked. Ribbon: dark green until 1941, when
white borders were added. The same medal is used for
RNVR decoration, which is only distinguished by its
ribbon: plain green until 1920, when a green central
stripe with two narrow red ones were added. Values
are in the same brackets.

  (a) ER VII or ERI D

  (b) GRV C

  (c) GRI or GRVI D

  (d) ER II E

122. ROYAL OBSERVER CORPS MEDAL (1950)

Obv. effigy of the reigning sovereign; rev.
Elizabethan coast watcher, legend THE ROYAL OBSERVER
CORPS MEDAL. Cupro-nickel. Ribbon: light blue with

central silver-grey stripe and narrow dark-blue
stripes on either side. Additional bars.

   (a) George VI, coinage head   D

   (b) Elizabeth II, coinage head, legend
       ELIZABETH II DEI GRA BRITT OMN
       REGINA F.D.   D

   (c) do., legend ELIZABETH II DEI GRATIA
       REGINA F.D.   C

123. THE CADET FORCES MEDAL (1950)

Obv. as above; rev. a torch with the legend CADET
FORCES MEDAL. Also in cupro-nickel. Ribbon: green
with yellow edges, narrow stripes of dark blue,
red and light blue.

   (a) George VI   D

   (b) Elizabeth II, 1st obv.   D

   (c) do., 2nd obv.   C

124. SPECIAL CONSTABULARY MEDAL (1918)

Obv. reigning sovereign; rev. FOR FAITHFUL SERVICE
IN THE SPECIAL CONSTABULARY. Ribbon: red central
stripe with white and black ones on the sides.

   (a) George V, crowned bust   B

   (b) do., with bar THE GREAT WAR
       1914-18 (Illustration No. 52) B

   (c) George VI, coinage head   B

   (d) do., without IND IMP   B

   (e) Elizabeth II, 1st obv.   B

   (f) do., 2nd obv.   B

Bars with legend LONG SERVICE and year are awarded
for further periods of service.

125. <u>COLONIAL POLICE LONG SERVICE MEDAL</u> (Illustration
     No. 51)

     Obv. effigy of the reigning sovereign; rev. a
     truncheon through a wreath with the legend COLONIAL
     POLICE : FOR LONG SERVICE AND GOOD CONDUCT. Ribbon:
     central green stripe with thin white stripes and
     wider dark-blue ones.

       (a)   George VI, without <u>IND IMP</u>   D

       (b)   Elizabeth II, 1st obv.   D

       (c)   do., 2nd obv.   D

126. <u>ST JOHN'S AMBULANCE BRIGADE LONG SERVICE MEDAL</u> (1898)

     Obv. Queen Victoria's effigy; rev. royal arms
     surrounded by the garter and motto, four circles with
     imperial crown, Prince of Wales' feathers and badges
     of the order. Alternate black and white stripes.

       (a)   silver, ring suspension   C

       (b)   silver, straight bar suspension   C
          (Illustration No. 28)

       (c)   silver-plated, straight bar
          suspension   B

     Bars are awarded for additional service.

127. <u>ORDER OF ST JOHN 1888</u> (Illustration No. 27)

     The insignia feature basically the Maltese cross
     with various embellishments according to the class.
     Ribbon: black moire.

       (a)   Bailiff Grand Cross, sash badge and
          star   I

       (b)   Dame Grand Cross, do.   H

       (c)   Knight of Justice, neck badge and
          star   F

       (d)   Dame of Justice, breast badge and
          star   F

(e)	Knight of Grace, neck badge and star	F
(f)	Dame of Grace, breast badge and star	F
(g)	Commander (Brother), neck badge	E
(h)	Commander (Sister), breast badge	D
(i)	Officer (Brother), do.	D
(j)	Officer (Sister), do.	D
(k)	Serving Brother, breast badge	D
(l)	Serving Sister, breast badge	D

128. <u>TURKISH MEDAL FOR THE CRIMEAN WAR 1854-5</u> (Illustration No. 22)

Silver circular medal. Obv. Sultan's cipher with legend <u>CRIMEA</u> in Turkish with date; rev. field gun with trophy of arms and flags of Turkey, England, France and Italy. Legend at the base <u>CRIMEA 1855</u> in French, Italian and English. Ribbon: deep red with green edges.

(a)	English: <u>CRIMEA 1855</u>, English flag to the fore, named or unnamed	C
(b)	French: <u>LA CRIMEE 1855</u>, French flag to the fore, unnamed	C
(c)	Italian: <u>LA CRIMEA 1855</u>, Italian flag to the fore, named or unnamed	C

The Italian medal was in fact issued to some of the British troops instead of the English one.

INDIA

1. MOST EXALTED ORDER OF THE STAR OF INDIA (1861)

    (a) Knight Grand Commander (GCSI), collar and
         chain   seldom offered for sale

    (b) Knight Grand Commander (GCSI), star and
         badge   L

    (c) Knight Commander (KCSI), 2nd Cl., star
         and neck badge   L

    (d) Companion (CSI), breast or neck
         badge   J

These were returnable on the death of the holder,
prior to 1947; since that date the holders have in
some cases been allowed to purchase the insignia,
with the exception of the chain of the Knight
Grand Commander (1st Cl.).

2. IMPERIAL ORDER OF THE CROWN OF INDIA (1878)

The badge consists of the royal and imperial
monogram in diamonds, turquoises and pearls. It is
rarely offered for sale and no recent valuation is
available.

3. MOST EMINENT ORDER OF THE INDIAN EMPIRE (1878)

Originally Companions only, but enlarged to three
classes in 1887. Same remarks as for No. 1 above,
regarding return and purchase of the insignia.

    (a) Knight Grand Commander (GCIE), collar
         chain   seldom offered for sale

(b) Knight Grand Commander (GCIE), star
     and badge   L

(c) Knight Commander (KCIE)   K

(d) Companion (CIE), breast badge, with
     INDIA on lotus flowers   I

(e) do., 2nd issue, without INDIA   I

(f) do., 3rd issue, smaller   G

(g) do., 4th issue, smaller neck badge   F

4.   <u>ORDER OF BRITISH INDIA</u> (1837)

In gold.

     (a) 1st Cl.   I

     (b) 2nd Cl. (slightly smaller)   G

5.   <u>INDIAN ORDER OF MERIT</u> (1837)

Star-shaped with REWARD OF MERIT and crossed swords
in centre. Ribbon: dark blue with red edges. Military
division values only given. There is also a civil
division.

     (a) 1st Cl., in gold (to 1912)   I

     (b) do., silver with gold centre
          (1912 to 1939)   G

     (c) do., but obv. changed to REWARD OF
          GALLANTRY instead of REWARD OF VALOUR
          as previously (1939-45)   I

     (d) as above, but with crown above legend
          (1945-7)   I

     (e) 2nd Cl., in silver with gold centre
          (1837-1912)   G

     (f) do., but in silver (1912-39)   F

     (g) do., obv. modified as for (c)
          (1939-45)   H

     (h) 3rd Cl., silver (1837-1912)   E

6.   <u>KAISAR-I-HIND MEDAL</u> (1900)

Obv. imperial cipher in the centre; rev. <u>KAISAR-I-HIND, FOR PUBLIC SERVICE IN INDIA</u>. Oval-shaped medal. <u>Ribbon: plain blue</u>. Bars could be awarded.

	1st Cl., gold	2nd Cl., silver	3rd Cl., bronze
Victoria	H	E	-
Edward VII	H	F	-
George V 1st issue	G	F	-
George V 2nd issue	G	F	F
George VI	I	G	G

7.   <u>INDIA DISTINGUISHED SERVICE MEDAL</u> (1907)

Obv. effigy of the reigning sovereign; rev. legend <u>FOR DISTINGUISHED SERVICE</u> within a wreath. Ribbon: blue, red, blue.

    (a) Edward VII   G

    (b) George V, 1st type   F

    (c) George V, 2nd type   F

    (d) George VI   F

8.   <u>INDIAN ARMY MERITORIOUS SERVICE MEDAL 1848-1947</u>

    (a) Honourable East India Company's MSM (1848-73) Obv. arms of the company with a trophy of arms; rev. recipient's name and unit with the legend <u>FOR MERITORIOUS SERVICE</u>   F

    (b) obv. Victoria veiled head (1889-1901); rev. lotus leaves and flowers, <u>INDIA</u> and <u>FOR MERITORIOUS SERVICE</u>   C

    (c) obv. Edward VII, military bust; rev. as above   D

    (d) obv. George V, crowned military bust; rev. as above   D

           (e)   obv. George VI, crowned head; rev. as
                 above   F

9.   INDIAN LONG SERVICE AND GOOD CONDUCT MEDAL

           (a)   Honourable East India Company 1848-73
                 Obv. as 8 (a) above; rev. as 8 (a) but
                 with legend FOR LONG SERVICE AND GOOD
                 CONDUCT   F

           (b)   Victoria diademed head VICTORIA REGINA
                 on obv. (1859); rev. crown and anchor
                 with legend FOR LONG SERVICE AND GOOD
                 CONDUCT   C

           (c)   Victoria veiled and diademed head, legend
                 VICTORIA KAISAR - I - HIND on obv. (1888-
                 1901); rev. lotus leaves and flowers with
                 legend INDIA and FOR LONG SERVICE AND
                 GOOD CONDUCT   B

           (d)   Edward VII, military bust; rev. as above
                 (1902-10)   C

           (e)   George V, military bust; rev. as above
                 (1911-30)   C

           (f)   do., without V after GEORGIUS in legend
                 on obv. (1930-6)   C

           (g)   George VI, crowned head; rev. as above
                 (1937-49)   C

Nos. 8 and 9 are silver medals, and the ribbon is
the same: plain crimson up to 1916, and for No. 8,
after 1916, crimson with a centre white stripe, for
No. 9, crimson with white edges after 1916. 8 (a),
9 (a) and (b) were awarded to European soldiers in
the Indian Army, the remainder to native soldiers.

10.   INDIAN AUXILIARY AND VOLUNTEER FORCES DECORATION
      1894-1930

Oval-shaped silver medal. Obv. imperial cipher with
the legend INDIAN VOLUNTEER FORCES; rev. name and
unit of recipient. Ribbon: plain green.

           (a)   Victoria, VRI (1892-1902)   D

140

     (b) Edward VII, ERI (1902–1910) D

     (c) George V, GRI (1902–1930)   C

11. EFFICIENCY MEDAL (1930–47)

Oval-shaped silver medal with a bar attached to the
fixed suspender with INDIA. Obv. reigning sovereign;
rev. FOR EFFICIENT SERVICE. Ribbon: green with yellow
edges. Bars are awarded for further service.

     (a) George V, crowned bust (1930–6)   C

     (b) George VI, crowned bust (1937–47)   C

12. VOLUNTEER LONG SERVICE MEDAL 1894–1930

Details of this medal are given under Great Britain
except that what follows was used in India only.
Obv. Edward VII, military bust, with legend EDWARDUS
VII REX ET IMPERATOR; rev. laurel branches with the
legend FOR LONG SERVICE IN THE VOLUNTEER FORCE.
Silver. Ribbon: plain green   B

13. INDIAN SERVICE MEDAL 1939–45 (Illustration No. 63)

Circular, cupro-nickel, unnamed. Obv. crowned head
of George VI with legend GEORGIUS VI D : G : BR :
OMN : REX ET INDIAE IMP; rev. map of India with
legend INDIA and dates 1939–45. Ribbon: dark blue
with central and two other light-blue stripes   A

14. INDIA INDEPENDENCE MEDAL (1949)

Circular, cupro-nickel, unnamed. Obv. imperial crown
and Ashoka's Chakra (wheel-shaped) with legend
GEORGIUS VI D : G : BRITT : OMN : REX : FID : DEF :;
rev. Ashoka's three lions, legend INDIA INDEPENDENCE
15TH AUGUST 1947. Ribbon: three equal vertical
stripes in saffron, white and green   B

REPUBLIC OF INDIA (from 1947)

15. PARAM VIR CHAKRA

Highest decoration for valour. Bronze circular medal.

Obv. four replicas of Indra's Vajra with the state
emblem in the centre; rev. legend PARAM VIR CHAKRA
in both Hindi and English with lotus flowers.
Ribbon: plain purple   no valuation available

16.   MAHAVIR CHAKRA

Second highest decoration awarded for acts of
conspicuous gallantry. Circular silver medal. Obv.
five-pointed heraldic star with domed centrepiece
bearing the gilded state emblem in the centre; rev.
legend MAHAVIR CHAKRA in both Hindi and English with
lotus flowers. Ribbon: half-white, half-orange   F

17.   VIR CHAKRA

Third highest decoration awarded for acts of
gallantry. Circular silver medal. Obv. five-pointed
heraldic star with a chakra in the centre, within a
domed centrepiece bearing the gilded state emblem;
rev. legend VIR CHAKRA in both Hindi and English and
lotus leaves   E

18.   ASHOKA CHAKRA

For gallantry other than in face of the enemy, awarded
in three classes:

        (a)   1st Cl., gilt gold, circular medal. Obv.
              Ashoka's Chakra, surrounded by lotus wreath,
              around which is a pattern of flowers and
              leaves; rev. legend ASHOKA CHAKRA in both
              Hindi and English with lotus flowers.
              Ribbon: green ribbon with central vertical
              orange stripe   G

        (b)   2nd Cl., circular silver medal with same
              design as 1st Cl., but ribbon is green
              with two vertical orange stripes   F

        (c)   3rd Cl., circular bronze medal with again
              same design as 1st Cl., and same ribbon but
              three vertical orange stripes   D

19. GENERAL SERVICE MEDAL (1947)

Circular medal, cupro-nickel. Always awarded with a
clasp. Obv. representation of Bhavani (Divine Sword);
rev. lotus flower with buds and leaves, and the
legend INDIA and GENERAL SERVICE MEDAL and date 1947.
Ribbon: red with five vertical green stripes.
Clasps: JAMMU AND KASHMIR 1947-48; OVERSEAS KOREA
1950-53   valuation for either   C

20. TERRITORIAL ARMY DECORATION

Oval-shaped silver medal. Obv. lotus wreath, a five-
pointed star in gold gilt and the state emblem in
gold; rev. lotus flower, buds and leaves embossed in
the centre. Medal worn from a silver bar brooch with
the legend TERRITORIAL. Ribbon: blue, orange and
white   C

21. TERRITORIAL ARMY MEDAL

Silver oval-shaped medal. Obv. state emblem; rev.
inscription ACHCHI SEVA KE LIYE in Devanagari.
Ribbon: dark blue with one orange and four white
vertical stripes   C

IRELAND

1. <u>1916 MEDAL</u>

    Obv. Cuchulainn, Irish hero; rev. 1916 and legend
    <u>SEACTMAIN NA CASGA</u>. Star-shaped, bronze, unnamed,
    but sometimes named privately. Ribbon: half-green,
    half-orange   E

2. <u>SERVICE MEDAL 1917-1921</u> (Illustration No. 64)

    Obv. soldier, four coats of arms and legend <u>EIRE</u>;
    rev. plain. Bronze, issued unnamed, but sometimes
    named privately   C

    The same medal with bar <u>COMRAC</u> issued to those
    who took part in military operations between
    1.4.1920 and 11.7.1921   D

    Named medals are at the upper part of the
    indicated price bracket for Nos. 1 and 2.

3. <u>MILITARY MEDAL FOR GALLANTRY 1944</u>

    Obv. cross with laurel wreath and St Brendan's knot.
    Legend <u>DE BARR CALMACTA</u>; rev. legend <u>AN BONN MILEATA
    CALMACTA</u>. Bronze. Ribbon: dark green with crimson
    stripe at each edge. Named. This medal is very rare
    and, as it has not been offered for sale yet, no
    value can be indicated.

4. <u>DISTINGUISHED SERVICE MEDAL</u> (1964)

    Obv. warrior standing in war chariot; rev. legend
    <u>AN BONN SEIRBHISE DEARSCNA</u>. Three classes, the first
    in silver (hallmarked), the others bronze. Ribbon:
    1st Cl. green with black centre stripe; 2nd Cl.
    green with black edge stripes; 3rd Cl. black edges

and black centre stripe. Only a small number of
these medals have been issued, mainly in 2nd and 3rd
Cl. Their value is estimated at   I

5.   <u>EMERGENCY SERVICE MEDALS 1939-1946</u> (Illustration
     No. 65)

     Obv. allegorical figure of Eire with legend <u>RE NA
     PRAINNE</u>; rev. a spray of laurel with dates <u>1939</u> and
     1946. Different legend for each of the services as
     indicated below. Bronze. Ribbon: two types (a)
     reddish orange with two white stripes (b) reddish
     orange with one white centre stripe. Bars were
     awarded for each additional two years' service after
     the qualifying period, with a maximum of two bars.
     These are in bronze with the dates 1939-1946 and a
     laurel spray. Issue unnamed. Bars do not affect the
     value.

          (i)   The Defence Forces (<u>NA FORSAI COSANTA</u>),
                 ribbon (a) (Illustration No. 66)   B

          (ii)   The Maritime Inscription (<u>AN SLUA MUIRI</u>),
                 ribbon (a)   B

          (iii) 26th Battalion (26u <u>CATHLAN</u>), ribbon
                 (a)   E

          (iv)   The Local Defence Force (<u>AN FORSA COSANTA
                 AITIUIL</u>), ribbon originally (b) changed
                 later to (a)   B

          (v)   Second Line Volunteer Reserve (<u>FORSA NA
                 NOGLACH 2u LINE</u>). ribbon (b)   B

          (vi)   The Army Nursing Service (<u>SEIRBHIS
                 ALTRANAIS AN ARM</u>), ribbon (b)   D

          (vii) The Chaplaincy Service (<u>AN SEIRBHIS
                 SEIPLINEACHTA</u>), ribbon (b)   E

          (viii) Volunteer Aid Division, Irish Red Cross
                 (<u>RANNA CABHAIR DEONT ACA CUMANN CROISE
                 DEIRGE NA H-EIREANN</u>), ribbon (b)   D

          (ix)   First Aid Division, Irish Red Cross
                 (<u>RANNA CEAD CABHRAC CUMANN CROISE DEIRGE
                 NA H-EIREANN</u>), ribbon (b)   D

(x)   Air Raid Precautions Organisation (NA
      SEIRBHISE REAMHCURAIM IN AGHAIDH AER-
      RUATHAR), ribbon (b)   B

(xi) Local Security Force (CAOMNOIRI AITIULA),
      ribbon (b)   B

6.   MERCHANT MARINE MEDAL 1939-1946

Obv. same as for the previous medals; rev. steamship
with legend AN TSEIRBIS MUIR-TRACTALA and the dates
1939-1946. Bars were issued at the same time as for
No. 5, but up to three could be awarded. Bronze.
Ribbon: blue with a white centre stripe. Issued
unnamed   F

7.   SERVICE MEDAL (1944)

Obv. Eire placing a laurel wreath on the head of a
kneeling soldier; rev. THE SERVICE MEDAL. Bronze
alloy. Ribbon: ten years' medal, plain blue ribbon.
Fifteen years' medal the same with gold centre
stripe. The ten years' medal is without bar and the
fifteen has a bronze bar.

     (a) 10 years' medal   D

     (b) 15 years' medal   E

8.   RESERVE DEFENCE FORCES SERVICE MEDAL (1961)

Obv. ancient Irish soldier on foot with legend FAIRE
BIODGAC TUS NA SAOIRSE; rev. legend AN BONN
SEIRBHISE - F.C.A. - S.M. and name of recipient.
Bronze. Ribbon: seven years' medal, blue with gold
edge stripes, and for the twelve years' medal
additionally a centre gold stripe. The seven years'
medal is without bar and the twelve has a bronze bar
of the same type as No. 7 above. Either   D

9.   1916 SURVIVORS' MEDAL (1966)

Obv. as for No. 1; rev. legend 1916 CAISC 1966.
Silver gilt. Ribbon: green with orange edges and a
white centre stripe. Unnamed   F

10. <u>ST JOHN AMBULANCE BRIGADE OF IRELAND SERVICE MEDAL</u>
     (1945)

Obv. <u>THE SAINT JOHN AMBULANCE BRIGADE OF IRELAND</u>
round a Maltese cross; rev. <u>FOR SERVICE</u> in a wreath.
Silver. Hallmarked. Ribbon: white with a black
centre stripe, a narrow black stripe on each side
and green edge stripes. For fifty years' service,
the same medal is issued in silver gilt.   C

Irish medals are issued with a straight pin-back
brooch, from which they are suspended. The design
varies according to the medal, but without it the
medal is not complete and is therefore worth less.

ITALY

1. <u>ORDER OF THE ANNUNZIATA</u> (1362)

Worn as a collar, this order was seldom awarded
except to members of royal familes or heads of state,
and therefore it is rare and there is no recent
valuation.

2. <u>ORDER OF ST MAURICE AND ST LAZARUS</u> (1434)

The badge is a green Maltese cross with gold edging,
with gold balls on the points and surmounted by an
enamel cross in white with gold edges. The first
four classes are surmounted by the royal crown.

      (a)   1st Cl., Knight Grand Cross, gold and
enamel sash badge and star   J

           do., but silver gilt   H

      (b)   2nd Cl., Knight Commander, neck badge
and breast star, gold and enamel   I

      (c)   3rd Cl., Commander, gold and enamel neck
badge   F

      (d)   4th Cl., Officer, gilt and enamel breast
badge   D

      (e)   5th Cl., Knight, gilt and enamel breast
badge   C

3. <u>MILITARY ORDER OF SAVOY</u> (1815)

This order underwent many changes in 1855, 1857,
1861 and 1869. When Italy became a republic during
WW II, the order became the Order of Military Merit
of Italy, and the letters R.I., for Republica
Italiana, appeared in the centre instead of the

cross. The badge is an Urdé cross, enamelled white
with gold edges, on a green enamelled laurel wreath.
The white cross of Savoy with an inscription round
it on a red circular band is in the centre on a.
circular plaque, edged with gold. The royal crown
is above the insignia of the 1st, 2nd and 3rd Cl.

    (a)   1st Cl., Knight Grand Cross, silver and
          enamel badge and breast star   H

    (b)   2nd Cl., Knight Commander, silver and
          enamel neck badge and breast star   G

    (c)   3rd Cl., Commander, silver and enamel
          neck badge   E

    (d)   4th Cl., Officer, gilt and enamel breast
          badge   D

    (e)   5th Cl., Knight, silver and enamel breast
          badge   C

4.   <u>ORDER OF THE CROWN OF ITALY</u> (1868)

The badge is a gold cross pattée, enamelled white
with gold edges, with love knots in gold between the
arms of the cross. The iron crown is in the centre
on a blue background.

    (a)   1st Cl., Knight Grand Cross, silver and
          gold sash badge and star   H

    (b)   2nd Cl., Knight Commander, neck badge and
          breast star   F

    (c)   3rd Cl., Commander, neck badge, gold and
          enamel   E

    (d)   4th Cl., Officer, breast badge, gilt and
          enamel   D

    (e)   5th Cl., Knight, breast badge, silver and
          enamel   C

5.   <u>MEDAL FOR MILITARY VALOUR</u> (1833)

Awarded in gold, silver and bronze with the same
design. Obv. arms of the House of Savoy and two
sprays with the crown above, and the legend <u>AL VALORE</u>

MILITARE round; rev. has laurel wreaths, with the
name of the recipient inscribed in the middle.
Ribbon: blue moire.

    (a) gold medal   rare, no recent valuation

    (b) silver   C

    (c) bronze   C

There is a variation of this medal, which has same
obv., but on rev. the legend SPEDIZIONE D'ORIENTE
and the dates 1855-1856 have been added and this
medal was issued for the Crimean War in silver. It
is rarer than the usual issue   E

6.   MEDAL FOR MILITARY VALOUR AFRICA 1936-7

Obv. coat of arms of the Royal Carabiniere with the
legend ARMA DEI REALI CARABINIERI NEI SECOLI FEDELE;
rev. MED. ARGENTO VALOR MILITARE. Ribbon: as above
C

7.   MEDAL FOR AERONAUTICAL VALOUR

Issued in gold, silver and bronze. Obv. (1st type)
effigy of King Victor Emmanuel III with the legend
VITTORIO EMANUELE III RE D'ITALIA and on the rev.
flying eagle and crown, and the legend MEDAGLIA
MILITARE AERONAUTICA. Obv. (2nd type) coat of arms
of the House of Savoy with a flying eagle, a crown
above, and the legend AL VALORE AERONAUTICA.

    (a) gold medals   rare, no recent valuation

    (b) silver, either type C

    (c) bronze, either type C

8.   WAR CROSS 1915-18

Bronze cross. Obv. MERITO DI GUERRA surmounted by
the royal cipher V E III and the royal crown, below
a Roman sword and sprays; rev. a star in the centre
of the cross. Ribbon: blue with two white stripes B

9.   WAR CROSS FOR THE SPANISH WAR 1936

Bronze cross. Obv. the arms of Spain with the legend
GUERRA POR LA UNIDAD NACIONAL ESPANOLA and arrows
below; rev. date 17-VII-1936. Although of Spanish
origin, it was widely distributed to the Italian
troops taking part in the Spanish Civil War   B

10.   WAR CROSS 1939-45

After 1943, the same cross as No. 8 was awarded but
R.I. (Republica Italiana) replaced the royal cipher
and the crown was removed   B

11.   CROSS OF MILITARY VALOUR 1915-18 and 1939-45

Similar cross to No. 8 and No. 10, but with inscription CROCE AL VALORE MILITARE. Ribbon: same.

          (a)   silver   C
          (b)   bronze   B

12.   COMMEMORATIVE MEDAL FOR THE 1914-18 WAR

Bronze. Obv. effigy of Victor Emmanuel III wearing
a helmet, legend GUERRA PER L'UNITA D'ITALIA 1915-
1918; rev. Winged Victory, legend CONIATA NEL BRONZO
NEMICO. Ribbon: green, white and red (Italian colours)
stripes   B

13.   VICTORY MEDAL 1915-18 (Illustration No. 5)

Bronze medal with Winged Victory on the obv., and the
usual rainbow ribbon   A

14.   MESSINA EARTHQUAKE MEDAL 1908 (Illustration No. 4)

Silver circular medal. Obv. effigy of Victor Emmanuel
III; rev. wreath of oak leaves, legend in the centre
MEDAGLIA COMMEMORATIVA — TERREMOTO CALABRO-SICULO —
28 DICIEMBRE 1908. Ribbon: white with two green
stripes   C

The same medal exists in gold and is much rarer   G

15. <u>CAMPAIGN AGAINST FRANCE 1940</u>

Bronze medal. Obv. Prince Umberto with legend
<u>UMBERTO DI SAVOIA — PRINCIPE DI PIEMONTE</u>; rev.
flying angel with a shield and the inscription
21.22.23.24 <u>GIUGNO—A—XVIII</u>, a mountain range and
legend <u>BATTAGLIA DEL FRONTE ALPINO OCCIDENTALE</u>.
Ribbon: narrow red and white stripes   B

16. <u>CAMPAIGN AGAINST FRANCE 1940</u>

Another medal with the same rev., and ribbon and, on
the obv. Italian soldier on a mountain with the
legend <u>VINCERE</u>   B

LUXEMBOURG

1. <u>ORDER OF THE OAK CROWN</u> (1841)

    Four-armed cross in white enamel with gold edge, on
    a wreath of oak leaves and acorns in gold. In the
    centre, on a green background, the letter W surmounted
    by a crown. There are the following classes:

(a)	Grand Cross, breast star	I
(b)	Grand Officer, neck badge	G
(c)	Commander, neck badge	F
(d)	Officer, breast badge	D
(e)	Knight, breast badge	D
(f)	silver-gilt medal	C
(g)	silver medal	B
(h)	bronze medal	B

    The last three medals are octagonal with the cross
    of the order on the obv. and an oak wreath on the
    rev. Ribbon: yellow with three green stripes.

2. <u>MILITARY MEDAL</u> (1945)

    Obv. effigy of the Grand Duchess with the legend
    <u>CHARLOTTE GRANDE DUCHESSE DE LUXEMBOURG</u>; rev. date
    1940 with the Luxembourg coat of arms and surmounted
    by a crown. The medal is in bronze and hangs from a
    dark-blue ribbon with three yellow vertical stripes
    C

3. <u>CROSS OF HONOUR AND MILITARY MERIT</u> (1951)

    Obv. heraldic lion on a shield in the centre with
    legend <u>HONOR, VIRTUS, PATRIA</u>; rev. letters CC

surmounted by a crown. Ribbon: blue with three
vertical white and red stripes. Three classes (a)
silver gilt (b) silver (c) bronze   all C

4.   CROIX DE GUERRE 1940-5

Bronze cross with two crossed swords and surmounted
by a crown, with the letter C on the obv. and the
date 1940 on the rev. Ribbon: dark blue with five
yellow stripes   C

5.   CROIX DE GUERRE (1951)

As above without the date 1940 and with an oak wreath
instead   C

6.   VOLUNTEERS' MEDAL 1914-18 (1923)

Bronze circular medal on a cross with two crossed
swords. Obv. seal of John the Blind with the legend
LUXEMBURGEM VIRTUTI; rev. steel helmet, French-type,
with dates 1914-1918 and names of battles on the
arms of the cross. Ribbon: wavy white and blue
horizontal stripes with red edges   B

7.   VOLUNTEERS' MEDAL 1940-45

This medal is similar to the previous one, except the
dates 1940-1945, and the names of battles on the rev.
are different. The ribbon is the same   B

8.   SERVICE CROSS (1850)

This is essentially a long-service award which has
been modified on various occasions between 1859 and
1960. It is a cross embellished with swords, oak
leaves and in some cases surmounted by a crown. It
is awarded for officers with gold or silver crown;
other ranks in bronze and silver, and in silver with
a silver crown. Ribbon: orange with green edges   C

FEDERATION OF MALAYA

1. <u>FEDERATION OF MALAYA ACTIVE SERVICE MEDAL (PINGAT KHIDMAT BERBAKTI)</u> (Illustration No. 67)

Silver circular medal suspended from crossed palm leaves. Obv. arms of the Federation of Malaya; rev. outline map of the Malaysian peninsula. Ribbon: yellow in the centre with green on each side, in which there is a vertical blue stripe   D

NEW ZEALAND

1. NEW ZEALAND CROSS (1869)

    Silver Maltese cross with a gold star on each arm.
    A gold crown above the cross suspended to the
    ribbon by a V and bar attachment. Ribbon: plain
    crimson. Very rare   L

2. NEW ZEALAND LONG AND EFFICIENT SERVICE MEDAL

    Silver medal with the effigy of the reigning sovereign
    on the obv. (Victoria, Edward VII and George V).
    Ribbon: deep red with two central white stripes   E

3. NEW ZEALAND TERRITORIAL SERVICE MEDAL

    Silver. Obv. effigy of George V with the legend NEW
    ZEALAND TERRITORIAL 12 YEARS SERVICE; rev. Kiwi
    among ferns   E

4. LONG SERVICE AND GOOD CONDUCT MEDAL (MILITARY) (1930)

    Obv.

        (a) George V, military bust

        (b) George VI, crowned head

        (c) George VI, crowned head with IND : IMP
            omitted

        (d) Elizabeth II, crowned head

        (e) do., shortened legend ELIZABETH II DEI
            GRATIA REGINA F D

    Rev. FOR LONG SERVICE AND GOOD CONDUCT. Ribbon: deep
    red with white edges. Additional bars can be granted.
    The medal has a suspender with the legend NEW ZEALAND
    D

5.   <u>EFFICIENCY MEDAL</u> (1930)

Obv. five different ones as above; rev. <u>FOR EFFICIENT
SERVICE</u>. Silver. Ribbon: green with yellow edges,
suspended from fixed suspender with legend <u>NEW
ZEALAND</u>   E

6.   <u>NEW ZEALAND WAR SERVICE MEDAL 1939-45</u> (Illustration
No. 68)

Cupro-nickel circular medal with obv. George VI,
coinage head; rev. legend <u>FOR SERVICE TO NEW
ZEALAND 1939-45</u>. Ribbon: black with white edges   B

7.   <u>NEW ZEALAND MEMORIAL CROSS</u> (1946)

Cross in dull silver with a crown on the upper arm,
fern leaves on the others, G vi R cipher in the
centre, with a wreath of laurels behind the cross.
Ribbon: purple   C

NORWAY

1. <u>ORDER OF ST OLAF</u> (1847)

    Enamelled cross pattée with the Norwegian lion in
    the centre surmounted by a crown. Ribbon: red with
    blue and white vertical stripes on the edges.

       (a) 1st Cl. Grand Cross, silver breast star
           with gold and enamel centre and sash
           badge   I

       (b) 2nd Cl. Commander, silver-gilt enamel
           neck badge   H

       (c) 3rd Cl. Knight, 1st Cl., breast badge with
           rosette on ribbon   E

       (d) 4th Cl. Knight, 2nd Cl., do., plain
           ribbon   D

    These prices are for the later issues; the earlier
    ones, especially with gold insignia for the lower
    classes, are worth more.

2. <u>WAR CROSS</u> (1941)

    Bronze cross with the Norwegian lion within a shield,
    surmounted by a crown in the centre of the cross,
    which hangs from the ribbon by a wreath. Ribbon: red
    with central blue stripe with white edging   C

3. <u>WAR MEDAL</u> (1941)

    Bronze circular medal. Obv. effigy of the king with
    legend <u>HAAKON VII</u> and <u>ALT FOR NORGE</u>. Ribbon: red
    with yellow stripes   B

4.   <u>ST OLAF'S MEDAL</u> (1939)

Circular silver medal. Obv. effigy of King Haakon VII,
surmounted by a crown. Ribbon: as for the Order of
St Olaf. A silver spray of oak leaves can be awarded
for war services   C

5.   <u>KING HAAKON VII FREEDOM CROSS</u> (1945)

White enamel cross with gold edging, with H 7 and a
crown in the centre of the obv; rev. <u>ALT FOR NORGE</u>
with the date 7 <u>JUNI</u> 1945. Ribbon: <u>dark blue with</u>
<u>white stripe</u>   C

6.   <u>KING HAAKON VII FREEDOM MEDAL</u> (1945)

In bronze with the same legend as the cross and the
dates 1940–1945. Ribbon: plain dark blue   C

7.   <u>PARTICIPATION MEDAL 1940–5</u>

Circular bronze medal with the Norwegian lion on a
shield, surmounted by a crown and the dates 9 <u>APRIL</u>
1940 and 8 <u>MAI</u> 1945. Ribbon: broad red edges and
white centre with narrow blue stripes   B

PAKISTAN

1. <u>NISHAN - i - HAIDAN</u>

    This award is equivalent to a British Victoria Cross.
    Bronze five-pointed star suspended from a ring with
    ornamental clasp. Crescent and star in a wreath in
    the centre of the star; rev. plain. Ribbon: plain
    dark green   no recent valuation available

2. <u>HILAL - i - JURAT</u> (Moon of Bravery)

    Equivalent to a British Distinguished Service Order.
    Gold circular medal suspended from a ring with
    ornamental clasp. Obv. stylised flowers with crescent
    and star in the centre; rev. plain. Ribbon: red,
    green, red   no recent valuation available

3. <u>SITARAT - i - JURAT</u> (Star of Bravery)

    Equivalent to a British Military Cross. Silver
    pentagonal medal with star superimposed, suspended
    from ornamental clasp; rev. plain, unnamed. Ribbon:
    white, dark green and white   C

4. <u>SITARA - i - BASALAT</u>

    Silver seven-pointed ornamental star with crescent
    and star in the centre; rev. plain. Suspended from
    an ornamental clasp. Ribbon: dark blue, red and
    light blue   C

5. <u>TAMGHA - i - JURAT</u> (Bravery Medal)

    Equivalent to the British Distinguished Conduct Medal.
    Circular bronze medal suspended from an ornamental
    clasp. Obv. trophy of lances, swords and a field gun,
    within a wreath with the crescent and star in the

centre; rev. plain. Ribbon: half dark red and half
dark green with narrow white edges   C

6.   <u>TAMGHA - i - BASALAT</u>

Circular bronze medal suspended from an ornamental
clasp. Obv. crescent and star within a wreath; rev.
plain. Ribbon: pale blue, red and dark blue   B

7.   <u>TAMGHA - i - KIHIDMAT</u> (military division)

      (a)   1st Cl., gold, five-pointed star with a
          backing of rays, a star and crescent in
          a circle in the centre. Worn round the
          neck from a red ribbon with a central
          white stripe   no recent valuation

      (b)   2nd Cl., same as above but in silver and
          the ribbon is red with two white
          stripes   no recent valuation

      (c)   3rd Cl., same as above, but in bronze with
          three white stripes on the red ribbon   D

8.   <u>PAKISTAN MEDAL</u> (1948)

Nickel circular medal. Issued unnamed, but some are
found named. Obv. GviR cipher, surmounted by a crown
with the legend <u>GEORGIUS VI D : G : BR : OMN : REX</u>;
rev. Pakistan flag within a wreath with native
lettering. Ribbon: green with a narrow white
stripe   B

9.   <u>CONSTITUTION OF THE REPUBLIC MEDAL</u> (1956)

Nickel circular medal, suspended from ornamental
clasp. Obv. stylised native design within a wreath;
rev. dated 23rd MARCH 1956 in English, repeated in
Vidu and Bengali. Ribbon: white, black, red and
green vertical stripes   B

10.   <u>TAMGHA - i - DIFA</u> (1947) (Illustration No. 69)

General service medal. Circular nickel medal, unnamed.
Obv. crescent and star within a wreath; rev. plain.
Issued with the following clasps:

164

(a) <u>KASHMIR</u> 1948   B

(b) <u>DIR BAJAUR</u> 1960-62   B

(c) native script   B

11. <u>WAR STAR (SITARA - i - HARB)</u> 1965

Gilt seven-pointed star with two circles in the
centre, and native script within. Rev. plain, with
name, rank and number of recipient. Ribbon: black
with thin red vertical stripe   A

12. <u>TAMGHA - i - JANG (WAR MEDAL)</u> 1965

Unnamed   B

13. <u>COMBINED FORCES LONG SERVICE MEDAL</u> (Illustration
No. 70)

Circular nickel medal. Unnamed. Obv. emblems of the
three services, crescent and star in the centre;
rev. legend in native script. Ribbon: green in the
centre, with light blue, dark blue and red edges   B

PORTUGAL

1. <u>MILITARY ORDER OF THE TOWER AND SWORD</u> (1495)

    Although founded in 1459, the order was reinstituted
    in 1808 and again in 1832. The value of the insignia
    can vary a great deal according to the period, and
    the brackets are for cheaper specimens.

    (a) Great Cross, breast star, badge and
         collar   no recent valuation

    (b) Grand Officer, breast star and badge   H

    (c) Commanders, neck badge   E

    (d) Officers, breast badge   D

    (e) Knight, breast badge   C

    The badge is a five-pointed star in white enamel,
    edged in gold with a gold ball resting on a wreath
    of oak enamelled green, surmounted by a tower in
    gold. Ribbon: plain blue.

2. <u>CROSS OF MILITARY MERIT</u>

    Recently created order. White enamel cross suspended
    from a tower in gold or silver. Ribbon: dark red
    with white central stripe and narrow black ones.

    (a) silver breast star   E

    (b) neck badge, gilt and enamel   D

    (c) breast badge, 3rd Cl.   C

    (d) breast badge, 4th Cl.   C

3.   <u>MILITARY ORDER OF ST BENEDICT OF AVIZ</u> (1162)

Took its present form in 1789 as an order for
military and naval merit. Cross with ornamental ends,
enamelled green, edge gold. The star is of chased
silver and the badge is in the centre.

    (a)   Grand Cross, breast star   F

    (b)   Commander's neck badge   D

    (c)   breast badge, silver and enamel   C

4.   <u>MILITARY ORDER OF CHRIST</u> (1522)

Originally established in 1318, it became a distinct
Portuguese order in 1522 and was altered in 1789. An
enamelled red cross with a white cross within. Ribbon:
plain red.

    (a)   Great Cross and breast star   F

    (b)   Grand Officer, neck badge and breast
         star   F

    (c)   Commander, neck badge   D

    (d)   Officer, breast badge   D

    (e)   Knight, breast badge   C

5.   <u>ORDER OF ST JAMES OF THE SWORD</u> (1177)

Reorganised in 1789 and 1862. It used to be a
military order, but it is now bestowed for services
to Arts, Science and Letters. The centre cross is
in violet enamel resting on two palms in green
enamel and with a white band bearing an inscription.
The badge hangs from a laurel wreath. The collar is
given for all five classes, in gilt silver for the
first four (valuation G) and in silver for the 5th
(valuation F).

    (a)   breast star, with enamel centre F

    (b)   neck badge   E

    (c)   Officer, breast badge   C

    (d)   Knight, breast badge   C

6.   MEDAL FOR MILITARY VALOUR

Ribbon: alternate blue and white stripes.

    (a) 1st Cl., gilt cross, green enamel leaves,
         legend VALOR MILITAR   C

    (b) 2nd Cl., do., but silver cross   C

    (c) 3rd Cl., do., but bronze cross   B

7.   DISTINGUISHED SERVICE MEDAL

A silver medal with a knight in armour on the obv.,
the medal being suspended from a trophy of armour,
knight's helmet, crossed swords and shield. Ribbon:
vertical stripes of red and white alternating   B

8.   GOOD CONDUCT MEDAL

A circular medal with the legend on the rev.
MEDALHIA MILITAR — COMPORTAMENTO EXEMPLAR. The rev.
varies according to the period but I know of:

    (a) D. Luiz I, Rei de Portugal, 1863, with
         military bust

    (b) do., different bust, without decorations
         (Illustration No. 73)

    (c) D. Carlos I, Rei de Portugal 1891
         (Illustration No. 74)

    (d) Republic's head with legend REPUBLICA
         PORTUGUEZA 1910 (Illustration No. 76)

    (e) Portuguese coat of arms

Ribbon: green and white vertical stripes alternating.
There are three classes, according to the length of
service:

    (i)   gold   C or D, according to period

    (ii)   silver   B

    (iii) bronze   A or B, according to period

9. DISTINGUISHED SERVICES OVERSEAS

Similar to above. Ribbon: half-red and half-black.
The same remarks apply regarding types, and the
valuation is similar.

10. ASSIDUOUS SERVICES OVERSEAS

Similar to previous medals, but with legend ASSIDADE
DE SERVICIO NO ULTRAMAR. Similar valuation.

11. CAMPAIGNS OF 1826-34 (Illustration No. 72)

Obv. effigy of Don Pedro IV and Dona Maria II,
conjointed bust; rev. legend CAMPANHAS DA LIBERDADE
1826-1834. Numeral I in circle. Ribbon: half-red
and half-black   B

12. MOZAMBIQUE CAMPAIGN 1894-5 (Illustration No. 75)

Obv. effigy of Dona Isabel; rev. EXPEDICAO A
MOCAMBIQUE and dates 1894-1895. Ribbon: plain red
with three thin vertical black stripes. Bronze
medal   B

13. CAMPAIGNS OVERSEAS, INCLUDING WORLD WAR I

Circular medal with coat of arms in the centre and
crown above. Ribbon: green with two red stripes on
the edges. This medal covers a wide range of
campaigns for which bars were issued, but the average
price is   B

14. AS ABOVE BUT FOR NON-COMBATANT SERVICE

Similar medal with white ribbon with red edges.
Prices are similar.

15. VICTORY MEDAL FOR THE FIRST WORLD WAR (1919)

Obv. Liberty's head; rev. angel. Bronze. Ribbon:
same as the other WW I Victory medals   A

16. <u>MEDAL FOR PROMOTION FOR BRAVERY</u>

Five-pointed star with Portuguese coat of arms in
the centre, suspended from a ribbon with two wide
vertical red stripes and a central narrower blue
one   B

17. <u>DISABLED AND WOUNDED MEDAL</u>

Similar to above, suspended from a red ribbon with
two green stripes   B

RHODESIA

1. <u>LONG SERVICE AND GOOD CONDUCT MEDAL</u> (MILITARY) (1930)

    Silver medal hanging from a suspender with the words
    <u>NORTHERN RHODESIA</u>, or <u>SOUTHERN RHODESIA</u>, or <u>RHODESIA</u>
    or <u>RHODESIA AND NYASALAND</u>. However, each type of bar
    does not necessarily exist with each different obv.
    Ribbon: crimson with white edges. Obv. as follows:

(a)	George V, military bust	F
(b)	George VI, crowned head	F
(c)	do., without <u>IND IMP</u> in legend	F
(d)	Elizabeth II, <u>DEI GRA BRITT OMN</u> in legend	F

    Rev. <u>FOR LONG SERVICE AND GOOD CONDUCT</u>

2. <u>EFFICIENCY MEDAL</u> (1930)

    Oval silver medal, hanging from a suspender with
    name of country as above. Obv. as above; rev. <u>FOR</u>
    <u>EFFICIENT SERVICE</u>. Ribbon: green with yellow edges.
    Bars for additional service can be granted   F

3. <u>SOUTHERN RHODESIA SERVICE MEDAL 1939–45</u>   F

4. <u>SOUTHERN RHODESIA MEDAL FOR THE KOREAN WAR 1950–3</u>

    no valuation available

5. <u>RHODESIA ACTIVE SERVICE MEDAL</u>

    Obv. effigy of Cecil Rhodes; rev. coat of arms   E

SOUTH AFRICA

1. <u>DEFENCE OF KIMBERLEY STAR 1899-1900</u>

Bronze six-pointed star with a ball on each point.
Obv. coat of arms, with the legend <u>KIMBERLEY 1899-</u>
<u>1900</u>; rev. <u>MAYOR'S SIEGE MEDAL 1900</u>. Ribbon: black
and yellow with a band of red, white and blue   E

2. <u>CAPE COPPER COMPANY MEDAL 1902</u>

Issued in silver and bronze. Obv. miner with legend
<u>THE CAPE COPPER COMPANY LIMITED 1886</u>; rev. legend
<u>PRESENTED TO THE OFFICERS NON COMMISSIONED OFFICERS</u>
<u>AND MEN OF THE GARRISON OF OOKIEP IN RECOGNITION OF</u>
<u>THEIR GALLANT DEFENCE OF THE TOWN UNDER LT. COL.</u>
<u>SHELTON D.S.O. AGAINST A GREATLY SUPERIOR FORCE OF</u>
<u>BOERS APRIL 4TH TO MAY 4TH 1902</u>. Ribbon: dark-copper
colour with a green stripe in the centre   I

3. <u>ANGLO-BOER WAR MEDAL 1899-1902</u> (1920)

Silver medal with the arms of the Transvaal on one
side and of the Orange Free State on the other   G

4. <u>DECORATION FOR DISTINGUISHED SERVICE IN THE ANGLO-</u>
    <u>BOER WAR 1899-1902</u> (1920)

Silver medal similar in design to the above, but
with the legend <u>VOOR TROUWE DIENST</u>   G

5. <u>AFRICA SERVICE MEDAL</u> (1943) (Illustration No. 71)

Obv. map of Africa with legend <u>AFRICA SERVICE MEDAL</u>;
rev. springbok. Cupro-nickel circular medal. Ribbon:
orange with green and brown vertical stripes   C

6. <u>SOUTH AFRICAN MEDAL FOR WAR SERVICES 1939-46</u>

Circular silver medal. Obv. South African coat of
arms; rev. <u>FOR WAR SERVICES SOUTH AFRICA</u> and dates
1939-1945. <u>Ribbon: orange, white and blue</u>   D

7. <u>CASTLE OF GOOD HOPE DECORATION</u> (1952)

The most senior South African award. Worn round the
neck. Obv. five-pointed star with a raised centre
showing the arrival of Jan van Riebeek in Table Bay
with the legend <u>CASTLE OF GOOD HOPE DECORATION</u>; rev.
plain. Ribbon: <u>sea green - a bar can be awarded</u>
rare, no recent valuation

8. <u>VAN RIEBEEK DECORATION</u> (1952)

Silver gilt five-pointed star. Obv. effigy of Jan
van Riebeek with legend <u>DISTINGUISHED SERVICE</u>; rev.
royal cipher and South African coat of arms. Ribbon:
pale blue - a bar may be awarded   G

9. <u>VAN RIEBEEK MEDAL</u> (1952)

Same as above in silver, but the ribbon has a white
central stripe   F

10. <u>CROSS OF HONOUR (HONORIS CRUX)</u> (1952)

Silver gilt eight-pointed Maltese cross. Obv.
enamelled green and gold with, in the centre, the
colours of the South African flag, surrounded by a
red circle with the legend <u>HONORIS CRUX</u>; rev. royal
cipher and the South African coat of arms. Ribbon:
green with red edges with white vertical stripes in
between. Bars can be awarded   G

11. <u>LOUW WEPENER DECORATION</u> (1952)

Circular silver medal. Obv. mountain peak with the
legend <u>THABA BOSIGO</u> 1865 at the bottom, and round
the medal <u>LOUW WEPENER DECORATION DEKORASIE</u>; rev.
royal cipher and South African coat of arms. Ribbon:
orange and white vertical stripes alternating. A
silver bar may be awarded   H

12. STAR OF SOUTH AFRICA (1952)

A decoration made up of eight superimposed five-
pointed silver stars of different sizes; rev. royal
cipher and the South African coat of arms. Worn
round the neck. Ribbon: orange with three green
stripes   H

13. JOHN CHARD DECORATION (1952)

Oval-shaped silver decoration. Obv. hospital at
Rorke's Drift with the legend RORKE'S DRIFT 1879
underneath, and JOHN CHARD DECORATION - DEKORASIE
round; rev. royal cipher with the arms of South
Africa. The arm in which the recipient serves is
shown by a miniature brooch on the ribbon: crossed
swords for the army, an eagle for the air force and
an anchor for the navy   H

14. JOHN CHARD MEDAL (1952)

The same but in bronze   F

15. SOUTHERN CROSS MEDAL (1952)

Circular silver medal. Obv. dark-blue enamel centre
in relief with stars of the Southern Cross in silver,
surrounded by silver oak leaves; rev. royal cipher
and South African coat of arms. Ribbon: dark blue
with two central stripes of orange and white   F

16. UNION MEDAL

Obv. the Union of South Africa coat of arms in
coloured enamel with the legend UNION MEDAL; rev.
royal cipher and South African coat of arms. Ribbon:
orange, white and blue vertical stripes   D

17. KOREA MEDAL 1950-3

Silver circular medal. Obv. maps of South Africa and
Korea with the legend KOREA and VRYWILLGERS -
VOLUNTEERS; rev. South African coat of arms and
royal cipher. Ribbon: central broad stripe in pale
blue with dark-blue and orange stripes   G

176

18. <u>LONG SERVICE AND GOOD CONDUCT MEDAL (MILITARY)</u> (1930)

Circular silver medal, with <u>SOUTH AFRICA</u> bar fixed
to suspender. Obv. as follows:

     (a) George V, military bust

     (b) Geroge VI, crowned head

     (c) do., without <u>IND IMP</u>

     (d) Elizabeth II, crowned head, <u>BRITT OMN</u> in
         legend

Rev. legend <u>FOR LONG SERVICE AND GOOD CONDUCT</u>.
Ribbon: crimson with white edges. Bars may be
awarded for further service   D

19. <u>EFFICIENCY MEDAL</u> (1930)

Oval silver medal, suspended from a fixed suspender
inscribed <u>UNION OF SOUTH AFRICA</u>. Obv. as above; rev.
legend <u>FOR EFFICIENT SERVICE</u>. Ribbon: green with
yellow edges. Bars may be awarded for further service
D

SPAIN

1. <u>ORDER OF THE GOLDEN FLEECE</u> (1430)

The order has one class only and has been essentially
awarded to Spaniards of aristocratic origin, royal
families in Europe and heads of state. Very rare.

2. <u>ROYAL ORDER OF CHARLES III</u> (1771)

Holy figure within an oval in the centre of a
Maltese-type cross, with balls at each point of the
cross, fleurs de lis between the arms of the cross.
Blue and white enamel with gold. The ribbon of the
order is blue and white.

    (a) 1st Cl., Knight with collar   J

    (b) 2nd Cl., Knight Grand Cross, badge and
breast star   H

    (c) 3rd Cl., Commander with star   G

    (d) 4th Cl., Commander with neck insignia   E

    (e) 5th Cl., Knight with breast badge   D

3. <u>MILITARY CROSS OF ST FERDINAND</u> (1811)

Cross surmounted by a crown.

    (a) 1st Cl., breast star with laurel wreath F
             sash badge F

    (b) 2nd Cl., cross worn on the buttonhole
with breast star without laurel wreath H

    (c) 3rd Cl., do., but smaller G

    (d) 4th Cl., buttonhole cross without wreath E

    (e) 5th Cl., buttonhole cross with wreath E

4. <u>ORDER OF ST HERMENGILDE</u> (1814)

Cross surmounted by a crown, with St Hermengilde on horseback in the centre.

      (a) 1st Cl., Grand Cross, breast star   F
      (b) 2nd Cl., Commander, breast star   E
      (c) 3rd Cl., Knight, breast badge   C

5. <u>ROYAL AMERICAN ORDER OF ISABELLA THE CATHOLIC</u> (1815)

Cross similar to No. 2, in red and gold, with, in the centre, enamelled round badge with two pillars, motto <u>PLUS ULTRA</u> and two terrestial globes, one surmounted by a crown. Ribbon: yellow and white.

      (a) 1st Cl., Grand Cross, sash badge and
          star   H
      (b) 2nd Cl., Commander with star, neck badge
          and star   G
      (c) 3rd Cl., Commander without star, neck
          badge only   E
      (d) 4th Cl., Knight, breast badge   D
      (e) 5th Cl., silver cross of the order
          (since 1907)   C
      (f) bronze medal of the order   B

6. <u>ALBUHERA CROSS</u>

Silver and enamel cross surmounted by a wreath D

7. <u>SAN SEBASTIAN MEDAL</u> (1836)

Silver medals, issued with a number of bars which include: <u>HERNANI</u>, <u>ALZA</u>, <u>SAN SEBASTIAN</u>, <u>FONTERABRA</u>, etc   D (average price bracket)

8. <u>YRUN MEDAL</u> (1837)

Oval-shaped gold and enamel medal, with trophy suspension   H

9. <u>MOROCCAN CAMPAIGN MEDAL</u> (1860)

Round silver medal, superimposed on cross. Effigy of
Queen Isabella II on the obv.; name of battles on
the rev.   C

10. <u>CARLIST WAR MEDAL 1868-70</u> (1875)

Small silver medal with effigy of Alfonso XII on obv.,
legend on rev. <u>VALOR, DISCIPLINA, LEALTAD</u>. Ribbon:
yellow with red stripes   B

11. <u>CUBAN CAMPAIGN MEDAL 1895-8</u>

Bronze medal with gilt suspender crown. Ribbon:
purple and red vertical stripes   D

12. <u>CENTENARY OF THE DEFENCE OF GERONA MEDAL 1809</u> (1909)

Silver   C

13. <u>MEDAL FOR PEACE IN MOROCCO</u> (1927)

Oval silver medal with legend <u>PAZ</u>, dates 1909-1927
and <u>MARRUECOS</u> and view of Arab city. Eagle and crown
surmounting the medal. Ribbon: white with green, red
and orange thin vertical stripes on the edges. Star
on the ribbon   B

SWEDEN

1. <u>ORDER OF THE SERAPHIM</u> (1748)

The order has one class only. The insignia consist
of a chain made of seraphim's heads and patriarch
crosses in blue enamel, and a badge. The badge, like
the breast star, is an eight-pointed cross in gold
and white enamel with golden seraphim between the
arms, and in the centre, a cross, the letters <u>IHS</u>
and three small crowns on a dark blue background.
There is a crown above the badge. The ribbon of the
order is pale blue.

     (a) breast star, silver gilt and enamel I - J

     (b) chain   no recent valuation

2. <u>ORDER OF THE SWORD</u> (1748)

Senior Swedish military order, which has five classes:

     (a) Grand Cross, eight-pointed cross in white
          enamel with gold edging; small golden
          crowns between the arms, above two
          crossed swords surmounted by a crown. Three
          small crowns and a sword in the centre,
          on a blue background. Additional crossed
          swords below and single swords on the
          side. Ribbon: yellow, with a narrow blue
          edge. Sash badge and breast star, silver
          gilt and enamel   I

     (b) Grand Officer, breast star, as described
          above   H

     (c) Commander, neck badge   G

     (d) Officer, breast badge, as above, but
          without crossed swords below or single

swords on the sides. Gold and enamel   F
do., silver and enamel   D

    (e) Knight, silver and enamel   C

3.   <u>KING OSCAR II JUBILEE MEDAL</u> (1897)

Obv. King's effigy. Ribbon: pale blue. Silver
medal   C

4.   <u>KING OSCAR II'S GOLDEN WEDDING 1907</u>

Silver medal with the King and Queen's effigy on the
obv. Ribbon: pale blue with golden edges   C

5.   <u>CROWN PRINCE GUSTAV'S SILVER WEDDING 1906</u>

Silver medal with conjointed busts of the Prince and
Princess on the obv. Ribbon: pale blue with yellow
edges and central yellow stripe, red edged   C

6.   <u>KING GUSTAV'S 70TH BIRTHDAY 1928</u>

Silver medal with the King's effigy. Ribbon: pale
blue   C

7.   <u>KING GUSTAV'S 90TH BIRTHDAY 1948</u>

Similar to above. Ribbon: the same   C

8.   <u>MEDAL FOR BRAVERY IN THE FIELD OR AT SEA IN TIME OF
WAR</u>

Gold and silver medals with the legend <u>ILLIS QUORUM
MERVERE LABORES</u>. Ribbon: blue with yellow stripe at
the edges.

    (a) gold   rare
    (b) silver   E

UNITED NATIONS

1. <u>UNITED NATIONS KOREA MEDAL</u> (1950) (Illustration
No. 46)

Circular bronze medal. Obv. terrestial globe within
laurel wreath; rev. legend FOR SERVICE IN DEFENCE OF
THE PRINCIPLES OF THE CHARTER OF THE UNITED NATIONS.
Ribbon: multi-stripe blue and white with bar KOREA.
The legend on the rev. of the medal and the bar
KOREA were produced in the various languages of the
twenty-two countries who fought in the UN force.
As some contingents were very much smaller than
others, some foreign-language versions are rarer than
others. The price indicated is for the English and
French versions   B

2. <u>UN EMERGENCY FORCE MEDAL</u> (1957)

For service in the Gaza strip. Same obv., but with
UNEF above the globe; rev. legend IN THE SERVICE OF
PEACE. Ribbon: sand yellow with wide centre blue
stripe and green and blue stripes on the edges   C

3. <u>UNITED NATIONS MEDAL</u> (1959)

Whilst the previous medals had a suspender bar, this
one has a ring suspender. The obv. is as for Nos. 1
and 2, but with UN; rev. has the legend in English
IN THE SERVICE OF PEACE and it was issued as follows:

<u>(a) Operations in the Congo (1960-4)</u>

1st type, ribbon: UN-blue with narrow white stripe
near the edges, with a small bronze bar pinned to
the ribbon with the word CONGO   C

2nd type, ribbon: blue with green edges and a narrow
white stripe in between. Without a bar   C

(b)   Military Observer Group in India and Pakistan
      1965-6

Same medal but the colours of the ribbon are
different; varying shades of green in the centre,
white stripe near the edges and UN-blue edges   C

(c)   UN Truce Supervision Organisation in Palestine
      1958

Same medal, but UN-blue ribbon with narrow white
stripe near each edge. As (a) 1st type   C

(d)   UN Temporary Executive Authority in New Guinea
      (1962)

Same medal, but UN-blue ribbon with a centre band
of dark green, white and pale green   C

(e)   UN Force in Cyprus (1964)

Same medal; ribbon: white wide central stripe and
wide blue edges with narrow pale-blue stripes in
between   C

(f)   UN Yemen Observation Mission 1964-5

Same medal; ribbon: varying shades of brown in the
centre with blue edges   C

As these medals are unnamed and the same medal is
used for (a) to (e), the same valuation has been
given, although it is quite certain that (d) and (f)
are rarer than the others and that (a) and (e) are
the most common. As all these medals are manufactured
in different countries there are small differences
in design which do not affect the value.

UNITED STATES OF AMERICA

1. <u>MEDAL OF HONOUR</u> (1861)

The highest-ranking US decoration and the only one
worn round the neck by US military personnel. There
are three types:

(a) <u>Navy Medal of Honour</u>

Five-pointed bronze star 2⅛in dia., with Minerva
fighting Discord in the centre. There is an anchor
at the top of the star, and its ring is suspended
from a light-blue silk moiré ribbon behind a centre
square pad with thirteen stars in white in the form
of a triple chevron. This decoration is also awarded
to the Marine Corps and the Coast Guard. There have
been various modifications to the design over the
years, and the main types are as follows:

    (i)   Civil War, copies (no current valuation
           for original medals)   F

    (ii)   Spanish-American War, originals   J
                                    copies   F

    (iii) WW I, copies (no current valuation for
           original medals)   F

    (iv)   current, originals   I

(b) <u>Army Medal of Honour</u>

Gold-finished, five-pointed star 1^9/16in dia., with
head of Minerva in the centre with the inscription
<u>UNITED STATES OF AMERICA</u> round it. The star is
suspended from a bar inscribed <u>VALOR</u> and surmounted
by an eagle grasping laurel leaves and arrows. Rev.
of the bar is inscribed <u>THE CONGRESS TO</u>, followed
by the name of the recipient. The ribbon is the same

as for the Navy Medal. The main types are as follows:

    (i)   Civil War, originals, named   K
                          restrikes   H-I

   (ii)   Spanish-American War, restrikes I

 (iii)   current, originals   H-I

(c) Air Force Medal of Honour (1918)

Gold-finished, five-pointed bronze star 2in dia., in
the centre the head of the Statue of Liberty
surrounded by thirty-four stars. The star is suspended
from a trophy made up of a bar with the word VALOR
above a thunderbolt. Ribbon: same as for above two
medals   I

2.   DISTINGUISHED SERVICE CROSS (ARMY) (1918)

Bronze cross 2in high, in the centre of which is the
American eagle and below a scroll inscribed FOR
VALOR. The centre of the rev. is surrounded by a
wreath. Ribbon: red, white and blue   C

3.   CERTIFICATE OF MERIT (ARMY) (1905)

Enacted by Congress as a certificare in 1847, it was
only in 1905 that a medal was instituted to be worn
by the holders of the certificate. It was discontinued
in 1918, and from then until 1934 holders could have
the obsolete decoration replaced by No. 2 above,
which has replaced it entirely since 1934. Obv.
American eagle and legend VIRTUTIS ET AUDACIAE
MOMUMENTUM ET PRAEMIUM; rev. UNITED STATES ARMY, a
wreath and in the centre FOR MERIT. Bronze. Ribbon:
white and blue. Originals J;   restrikes F

4.   BREVET MEDAL (MARINE CORPS) (1921)

Issued to holders of brevet commissions granted for
distinguished services in the Mexican War, Civil
War, Spanish War, Philippine Insurrection, and the
Boxer Rebellion. Awarded to only twenty-three
officers. Bronze cross with centre medallion bearing
the legend BREVET surrounded by UNITED STATES MARINE
CORPS and on the rev. FOR DISTINGUISHED SERVICE IN

THE PRESENCE OF THE ENEMY. Ribbon: red moiré with
thirteen white stars. Originals K;   restrikes   I

5.   SPECIALLY MERITORIOUS MEDAL (1901)

Sometimes called Meritorious Service Medal. Issued
during the war with Spain to less than 100 officers
and men of the US Navy and Marine Corps. Bronze
cross pattée with medallion in the centre with the
inscription U.S. NAVAL CAMPAIGN WEST INDIES, laurel
and oak wreath, with an anchor within. On the arms
of the cross the inscription SPECIALLY MERITORIOUS
SERVICE 1898; rev. plain. Ribbon: bright scarlet.
Originals estimated K;   restrikes H. A few exist
with an inscribed bar.

6.   NAVY CROSS (1919)

Obv. sailing vessel over a circle in the centre of
the cross; rev. crossed anchors and the legend U.S.N.
Additional awards are shown by gold stars. Ribbon:
blue with white centre stripe   E

7.   AIR FORCE CROSS (1960)

Bronze cross 1^{5}/16in dia., with satin finish. In the
centre a gold-plated eagle with cloud formation
behind surrounded by a green-enamel laurel wreath.
Ribbon: blue with thin white and red stripes at the
edges   D

8.   DISTINGUISHED SERVICE MEDAL (1918)

(a) Army

Obv. coat of arms of the US surrounded by a blue-
enamel circle with the legend FOR DISTINGUISHED
SERVICE and MCMXVIII. Additional awards are shown by
bronze oak-leaf clusters. Ribbon: wide white central
stripe, thin blue stripes and red thicker stripes
on the edges   D

(b) Navy

Obv. gilded bronze with the US eagle in the centre
surrounded by the legend UNITED STATES OF AMERICA —

<u>NAVY</u>: rev. Neptune's trident with laurel wreath and
<u>the</u> legend FOR DISTINGUISHED SERVICE. Additional
awards are shown by gold stars. The medal is
surmounted by a white enamelled star with an anchor
in the centre. Ribbon: blue and yellow   F

(c) Air Force

Obv. thirteen gold rays and thirteen white enamel
stars with blue stone in the centre. Additional awards
are shown by bronze oak-leaf clusters. Ribbon: white,
blue and yellow   D

(d) Coast Guard

Circular gilded bronze medal with sailing vessel and
the legend <u>U.S. COAST GUARD</u> and <u>DISTINGUISHED SERVICE</u>.
Additional awards are shown with gold stars. Ribbon:
blue, white and purple   estimated H-I

9. <u>SILVER STAR MEDAL</u> (1918)

Originally a ^{3}/16in dia. citation star to be worn on
a campaign ribbon, it was changed to its present
design in 1932. Bronze star $1\frac{1}{4}$in dia., with on the
obv. a wreath with a ^{3}/16in dia. silver star in the
centre. Additional awards are shown by oak-leaf
clusters for the army and the air force and gold
stars for the navy and the coast guard   C

10. <u>LEGION OF MERIT</u> (1942)

Issued in four classes to the armed forces of foreign
countries friendly to the USA, and to US personnel
without class (legionnaire).

    (a) 1st Cl., Chief Commander, domed, five-
pointed American white star plaque
surrounded by red enamel, thirteen white
stars on blue field. 3in dia., with
<u>UNITED STATES OF AMERICA</u> on the rev.
Behind the star, laurel wreath with crossed
arrows   E

    (b) 2nd Cl., Commander, worn round the neck.
As above but with bronze wreath above;
rev. white enamelled star with a disc in

the centre bearing the legend ANNUIT
COEPTIS and MDCCLXXXII and UNITED STATES
OF AMERICA. $2\frac{1}{4}$in dia. Ribbon: purple red
with white edges   E

(c)   3rd Cl., Officer, smaller version of
above ($1\frac{7}{8}$in dia.) worn on the left breast
with small replica of the badge in gilt
bronze on the ribbon   D

(d)   4th Cl., Legionnaire, as above but without
replica on the ribbon   C

11.   DISTINGUISHED FLYING CROSS (1926)

Bronze cross with a four-bladed propeller superimposed.
Ribbon: blue with red centre stripe with white
edging, and two white stripes near the edges   C

12.   SOLDIER'S MEDAL (1926)

Octagonal bronze medal with an eagle with wings
displayed, standing on two groups of stars. On the
rev. the legends SOLDIER'S MEDAL and FOR VALOR
and sprays of laurel and oak. Bronze oak-leaf
clusters for additional awards. Ribbon: two broad
blue stripes with narrow red and white ones   B

13.   NAVY AND MARINE CORPS MEDAL (1942)

Octagonal medal in bronze with eagle with wings
displayed on an anchor and globe, below which the
legend HEROISM. Additional awards are shown by gold
stars. Ribbon: blue, gold and scarlet   D

14.   COAST GUARD MEDAL

Octagonal medal within which is a coil of rope
inside which is the Coast Guard coat of arms and
the inscription UNITED STATES COAST GUARD 1790.
Ribbon: three broad blue stripes and narrower white
and red ones   estimated H

15.   AIRMAN'S MEDAL (1960)

Circular bronze medal with obv. Hermes and American

eagle with the legend AIRMAN'S MEDAL; rev. laurel
wreath with the legend FOR VALOR. Ribbon: two broad
light-blue stripes and narrow dark-blue and yellow
stripes   B

16.   BRONZE STAR (1944)

Bronze star 1½in dia. with a ^{3}/16in raised bronze
star in the centre; rev. the legend HEROIC OR
MERITORIOUS ACHIEVEMENT. Ribbon: red with blue stripe
in the centre and four narrow white stripes.
Additional awards are shown by oak-leaf clusters for
the army and gold stars for the other services   B

17.   MERITORIOUS SERVICE MEDAL (1969)

Bronze medal 1½in dia., made up of six rays issuing
from the upper three points of a five-pointed star,
with an eagle in front and laurels; rev. the legend
UNITED STATES OF AMERICA MERITORIOUS SERVICE. Ribbon:
dark-red with white vertical stripes. Additional
awards are shown with oak-leaf clusters for the army
and gold stars for the other services   B

18.   AIR MEDAL (1942)

Bronze, shaped in the form of a compass rose, with
an eagle in flight superimposed; rev. centre plain.
As this medal can be awarded several times, there
are a number of devices which can be worn on the
ribbon, including a V when awarded for heroic deeds.
These do not greatly affect the value, but this
medal can be found with an additional length of
ribbon to carry the various devices   B

19.   JOINT SERVICE COMMENDATION MEDAL (1963)

Four hexagons of green enamel within a wreath, with
eagle superimposed and stars above. Ribbon: blue,
white and black   C

20.   ARMY COMMENDATION MEDAL (1945)

Originally the Commendation Ribbon and later the
Army Commendation Ribbon with medal pendant, it took

its present form in 1960. Additional awards are
shown by bronze oak-leaf clusters and the V device
can also be worn on the ribbon. Octagonal bronze
medal with the American eagle; rev. legend FOR
MILITARY MERIT. Ribbon: green and white   B

21. NAVY COMMENDATION MEDAL (1944)

Originally the Commendation Ribbon with medal
pendant. Additional awards are shown with gold stars,
while the V device can be worn on this medal ribbon
also. This medal is the same as No. 20 above, but
the ribbon is green with two vertical white stripes
B

22. COAST GUARD COMMENDATION MEDAL (1947)

Originally the Coast Guard Commendation Ribbon with
medal pendant. Hexagonal bronze medal with a coil of
rope inside, the American eagle within the rope and
the Coast Guard coat of arms in the centre, with
the legend UNITED STATES COAST GUARD 1790. Additional
awards are shown with gold stars. Ribbon: green and
white   H

23. AIR FORCE COMMENDATION MEDAL (1958)

Hexagonal bronze medal with an eagle and the coat of
arms of the branch of the air force; rev. the legend
FOR MILITARY MERIT and a space for the recipient's
name. Ribbon: yellow and blue vertical stripes   B

24. NAVY ACHIEVEMENT MEDAL (1960)

Originally only a ribbon called Navy Commendation
for Achievement. The V device can be worn on the
ribbon of this medal. Square medal in bronze with
four stars and an anchor. Ribbon: green with two
vertical red stripes   D

25. COAST GUARD ACHIEVEMENT MEDAL (1960)

Similar to above   F

26. <u>NATIONAL SECURITY MEDAL</u> (1953)

Primarily a civilian award, but also awarded to members of the forces. Blue enamelled compass rose, inside a red circle surrounded by a laurel wreath, with an eagle on top, and the legend <u>UNITED STATES OF AMERICA</u> and <u>NATIONAL SECURITY</u>. A serial number appears on the eagle on the rev., and the legend is <u>PRESENTED TO</u> with the name of the recipient inscribed. Ribbon: dark blue and gold with diagonal gold lines   I

27. <u>PURPLE HEART</u> (1932)

Originally the figure of a heart in purple cloth or silk, edged with narrow silver lace. Only a few were issued when instituted by George Washington, and it was only in 1932 that it was revived in the form of a medal. It has the shape of a purple heart, within a bronze border with a George Washington profile, above the general's coat of arms between green enamelled sprays; rev. the inscription <u>FOR MILITARY MERIT</u>. Additional awards are shown by bronze oak-leaf clusters for the army and gold stars for the other services. Ribbon: purple with white edge.

    (a) WW II type, enamel centre   C

    (b) current type, plastic centre   B

28. <u>MERCHANT MARINE DISTINGUISHED SERVICE MEDAL</u> (1942)

Bronze circular medal with silver star superimposed and eagle above. Ribbon: blue, white and red   I

29. <u>MERCHANT NAVY MERITORIOUS SERVICE MEDAL</u> (1944)

Bronze, in the shape of an eagle over an anchor. Ribbon: blue, with central narrow stripes of gold, red, white and blue   G

30. <u>MARINER'S MEDAL</u> (1943)

Bronze star with silver disc superimposed, showing

eagle and anchor. Ribbon: a broad red stripe, a
narrow white and a broad blue   E

31.   COMBAT READINESS MEDAL (1964)

Two triangles over concentric rays, in bronze.
Additional awards are shown with oak-leaf clusters.
Ribbon: red with vertical broad white and narrow
blue stripes   B

32.   ARMY GOOD CONDUCT MEDAL (1941) (Illustration No. 79)

Bronze circular medal with obv. eagle standing on a
closed book and sword, with the legend EFFICIENCY –
HONOR – FIDELITY; rev. five-pointed star and legend
FOR GOOD CONDUCT with wreath. Succeeding awards are
shown by bronze, silver and gold clasps. Ribbon: red
with vertical white stripes   A

33.   AIR FORCE GOOD CONDUCT MEDAL (1953)

Same design as above but with different ribbon:
blue with thin red, white and blue vertical stripes
A

34.   NAVY GOOD CONDUCT MEDAL (1892)

Originally created as a badge in 1869. Bronze
circular medal. Obv. sailing ship in the centre over
an anchor and surrounded by a circle of chain.
Legend CONSTITUTION, UNITED STATES and NAVY; rev.
legend FIDELITY, ZEAL, OBEDIENCE. The suspension was
in the form of a bar but has been changed to a ring
in recent years. Ribbon: plain red. Clasps used to
be given, but this is no longer the case.

        (a)   older type, bar suspender B

        (b)   older type, named   D

        (c)   current type   B

35.   MARINE CORPS GOOD CONDUCT MEDAL (1896)

Obv. Marine gunner and gun over anchor within a coil
of rope. Legend SEMPER FIDELIS; rev. legend FIDELITY,

ZEAL, OBEDIENCE. This medal has an unusual suspension
bar shaped as a miniature rifle. Ribbon: plain red
with central vertical blue stripe.

    (a) older type, with top brooch C

    (b) named or numbered D-F

    (c) current type B

36. COAST GUARD GOOD CONDUCT MEDAL (1923)

Obv. Coast Guard seal of crossed anchors with the
inscription UNITED STATES COAST GUARD 1790, with
crossed oars below, the whole within a coil of chain.
Ribbon: maroon with central white stripe. Additional
awards are shown with bronze stars.

    (a) large, old type D

    (b) current type C

37. AIR FORCE LONGEVITY SERVICE AWARD (1957)

Replaces the Federal Service stripes. Issued as a
ribbon only   no valuation

38. ARMED FORCES RESERVE MEDAL (1950)

Circular bronze medal with obv. a torch over crossed
powder horn and bugle within a circle of thirteen
stars; rev. has the legend ARMED FORCES RESERVE with
variations according to the service. Ribbon: white
and blue on which a device with an hour glass and X
is worn to show an additional ten years' service.
Valuations as follows:

    (a) Army (Minute Man) A

    (b) National Guard (National Guard insignia) B

    (c) Air Force (eagle) B

    (d) Navy (sailing ship and eagle) D

    (e) Marine Corps (Marine Corps insignia) D

    (f) Coast Guard (Coast Guard insignia) E

39. <u>NAVAL RESERVE MEDAL</u> (1938)

Obv. American eagle with anchor; rev. <u>UNITED STATES
NAVAL RESERVE</u> and <u>FAITHFUL SERVICE</u>. Ribbon: plain
red with thin blue and white edges. A bronze star
is awarded for a further ten years' service   C

40. <u>ORGANIZED MARINE CORPS RESERVE MEDAL</u> (1939)

Obv. a Marine and a civilian reservist, with the
legend <u>MARINE CORPS RESERVE</u> and <u>FOR SERVICE</u>; rev. is
the same as for the Marine Corps Good Conduct
Medal   D

41. <u>NAVY RESERVE MERITORIOUS SERVICE MEDAL</u> (1959)

Circular bronze medal with obv. anchor with the
inscription <u>MERITORIOUS SERVICE</u> surrounded by the
legend <u>UNITED STATES NAVY RESERVE</u>. Ribbon: two broad
red vertical stripes, three smaller blue ones and
two thin white ones   D

42. <u>NAVY EXPERT PISTOL SHOT MEDAL</u>

Circular medal with a smaller one superimposed, eagle
and anchor on the smaller one and a target on the
larger one, with the legend <u>UNITED STATES NAVY</u> and
<u>EXPERT PISTOL SHOT</u>. Ribbon: blue with two narrow
white stripes   D

43. <u>NAVY EXPERT RIFLEMAN MEDAL</u>

The same, but the legend reads <u>EXPERT RIFLEMAN</u> and
the ribbon has three narrow white stripes   D

44. <u>COAST GUARD EXPERT PISTOL SHOT MEDAL</u>

Medal in the shape of a shield with crossed pistols
and target and the legend <u>U.S. COAST GUARD EXPERT</u>.
Ribbon: blue with two thin stripes   D

45. <u>COAST GUARD EXPERT RIFLEMAN MEDAL</u>

Same design but with crossed rifles, and the ribbon
blue with four thin vertical stripes   D

46. DEWEY MEDAL (1898)

Obv. Commodore Dewey; rev. legend THE GIFT OF THE
PEOPLE OF THE UNITED STATES TO THE OFFICERS AND MEN
OF THE ASIATIC SQUADRON UNDER THE COMMAND OF
COMMODORE GEORGE DEWEY. Around the edge, the legend
IN MEMORY OF THE VICTORY OF MANILA BAY MAY 1, 1898,
and a small panel for the name of the ship on which
the medal was earned. The medal hangs by a ring from
a pendant and the ribbon hangs from the pendant
behind the medal.

     (a) original with ship name; name, rank
         and service inscribed on rim   J

     (b) do., to Marines   K

     (c) unnamed restrikes   I

47. ARMY CIVIL WAR MEDAL (1907)

Obv. head of Lincoln with the legend WITH MALICE
TOWARDS NONE, WITH CHARITY FOR ALL; rev. THE CIVIL
WAR and the dates 1861-1865 within a wreath.
Ribbon: half-blue and half-grey.

     (a) numbered on rim   J

     (b) later issues and restrikes without
         number   E

48. NAVY CIVIL WAR MEDAL (1908)

Obv. the battle between the USS Monitor and the
Confederate Merrimac; rev. anchor and chain with the
legend FOR SERVICE and UNITED STATES NAVY. The same
medal also exists with UNITED STATES MARINE CORPS
instead of USN. Ribbon: blue and grey.

     (a) USN   J

     (b) USMC   K

     (c) restrikes, not numbered F

49. <u>INDIAN CAMPAIGN MEDAL</u> (1907)

Obv. mounted Indian with legend <u>INDIAN WARS</u>; rev.
trophy with an eagle on a cannon and various arms,
and the legend <u>UNITED STATES ARMY</u> and <u>FOR SERVICE</u>.

    (a)   numbered   I

    (b)   not numbered, later issues and
           restrikes   E

50. NAVAL CAMPAIGN MEDAL FOR THE WEST INDIES 1898

Also known as the Sampson Medal. Obv. effigy of
Admiral William T. Sampson with the legend <u>U.S.</u>
<u>NAVAL CAMPAIGN WEST INDIES 1898</u> and <u>WILLIAM T.</u>
<u>SAMPSON</u> and <u>COMMANDER IN CHIEF</u>; rev. naval officer,
naval gunner and marine, with below a panel for the
name and date of the engagement. A bronze bar with
the name of the ship is worn on the upper part of
the ribbon. Ribbon: red, blue and red   F

51. <u>CHINA CAMPAIGN MEDAL (ARMY)</u> (1905)

Obv. imperial Chinese dragon with the legend <u>CHINA</u>
<u>RELIEF EXPEDITION</u> 1900-1901; rev. as for No. <u>49</u>
above. Ribbon: yellow with blue edges

    (a)   numbered   I

    (b)   not numbered, later issues and
           restrikes   D

52. <u>CHINA CAMPAIGN MEDAL (NAVY)</u> (1908)

Also known as the China Relief Expedition Medal.
Obv. pagoda with the legend <u>CHINA RELIEF EXPEDITION</u> -
1900; rev. eagle with open wings and naval anchor
with the legend <u>FOR SERVICE</u> and <u>UNITED STATES NAVY</u>
or <u>UNITED STATES MARINE CORPS</u>. Ribbon: yellow with
thin blue edges.

    (a)   Navy, numbered   I

    (b)   Navy, not numbered, restrikes F

        (c)   Marine Corps, numbered   J

        (d)   not numbered restrikes   F

53.   <u>PHILIPPINE CONGRESSIONAL MEDAL</u> (1906)

      Obv. three soldiers, one bearing a flag with the
      legend <u>PHILIPPINE INSURRECTION</u> and 1899; rev. legend
      <u>FOR PATRIOTISM, FORTITUDE AND LOYALTY</u> in a wreath.
      Ribbon: blue, red and white.

        (a)   numbered   E

        (b)   not numbered C

54.   <u>PHILIPPINE CAMPAIGN MEDAL (ARMY)</u> (1905)

      Obv. palm tree with lamp and scales; rev. as for No.
      49. Ribbon: blue with two broad red stripes.

        (a)   numbered   D

        (b)   not numbered C

55.   <u>PHILIPPINE CAMPAIGN MEDAL (NAVY)</u> (1908)

      Obv. old Manila gateway with the legend <u>PHILIPPINE
      CAMPAIGN</u> and the dates 1899–1903; rev. as for No. 52.
      Ribbon: as above.

        (a)   numbered   F

        (b)   not numbered, restrikes   D

        (c)   Marine Corps, rev. numbered   I

        (d)   do., not numbered, restrikes E

56.   <u>ARMY OF PUERTO RICO OCCUPATION MEDAL</u> (1919)

      Obv. castle with the legend <u>ARMY OF OCCUPATION,
      PORTO RICO</u> and <u>1898</u>; rev. as for No. 49. Ribbon: red
      blue and yellow.

        (a)   numbered   E

        (b)   not numbered, restrikes and
              re-issues   C

57. <u>ARMY OF CUBA OCCUPATION MEDAL</u> (1915)

Obv. Cuban Republic coat of arms with wreath and the
legend <u>ARMY OCCUPATION MILITARY GOVERNMENT OF CUBA</u>
and the dates 1898 and 1902; rev. as for No. 49.
Ribbon: blue, yellow and red.

    (a) numbered   E

    (b) not numbered, restrikes and re-issues C

58. <u>SPANISH WAR SERVICE MEDAL</u> (1918)

Obv. Roman sword in a sheath on a tablet with the
legend <u>FOR SERVICE IN THE SPANISH WAR</u>, surrounded by
a wreath; rev. US coat of arms with the badges of
the infantry, cavalry and artillery. Ribbon: green
and yellow.

    (a) numbered   D

    (b) not numbered, restrikes and re-issues C

59. <u>WEST INDIES CAMPAIGN MEDAL</u>

Obv. Morro Castle, Cuba, with the legend <u>WEST INDIES
CAMPAIGN 1898</u>. Ribbon: yellow and blue. Navy or
Marine Corps rev.   J

60. <u>SPANISH CAMPAIGN MEDAL (ARMY)</u> (1905)

Obv. castle within the legend <u>WAR WITH SPAIN</u> and the
date 1898; rev. as for No. 49. Ribbon: yellow and
blue.

    (a) numbered   E

    (b) not numbered, restrikes D

61. <u>SPANISH CAMPAIGN MEDAL (NAVY)</u> (1908)

Obv. as for No. 59 but with the legend <u>SPANISH
CAMPAIGN</u> and the date 1898; rev. as for No. 52.

    (a) numbered   F

    (b) restrikes   no recent offers

    (c) Marine Corps, numbered   I

62. ARMY OF CUBA PACIFICATION MEDAL (1909)

Obv. Cuban Republic coat of arms between two
American soldiers. Legend CUBAN PACIFICATION and the
dates 1906-1909; rev. as for No. 49. Ribbon: red,
white, blue and olive.

(a) numbered   D

(b) not numbered   C

63. NAVY CUBAN PACIFICATION MEDAL (1909)

Obv. Columbia wearing a sword in a scabbard, holding
a flag and an olive branch with a Cuban kneeling.
Legend FOR SERVICE; rev. UNITED STATES NAVY or
UNITED STATES MARINE CORPS. Ribbon: as above.

(a) Navy, numbered   D

(b) Marine Corps, numbered   E

(c) Navy, not numbered   C

(d) Marine Corps, not numbered D

64. NICARAGUAN CAMPAIGN MEDAL (1913)

Obv. Lake Managua and forest, with mountain, legend
NICARAGUAN CAMPAIGN and 1912; rev. eagle with spread
wings over an anchor, with the legend FOR SERVICE
and UNITED STATES NAVY or UNITED STATES MARINE CORPS.
Ribbon: red with two dark-blue stripes.

(a) Navy, numbered   I

(b) Navy, not numbered   E

(c) Navy, restrikes   D

(d) Marine Corps, numbered   I

(e) Marine Corps, not numbered F

(f) Marine Corps, restrikes   E

65. HAITIAN CAMPAIGN MEDAL (1917)

Three models:

(a)   with dates 1915–16

(b)   with dates 1915–16 and bar 1919–1920

(c)   with dates 1919–1920

Obv. a palm tree with a background of waves, shore
and mountains, legend HAITIAN CAMPAIGN and the dates
as indicated above; rev. eagle over naval anchor
and the legend as for No. 65 above. Ribbon: dark-blue
with two central red stripes.

(a)   numbered   G

(b)   restrikes   E

66.   DOMINICAN CAMPAIGN MEDAL (1921)

Obv. the Tower of Homage in Ciudad Trujillo; rev.
eagle on naval anchor and the legend FOR SERVICE
within laurel wreath. Ribbon: crimson with two blue
stripes.

(a)   Navy, numbered   H

(b)   Navy, not numbered   D

(c)   Marine Corps, numbered   G

(d)   Marine Corps, not numbered D

67.   ARMY MEXICAN SERVICE MEDAL (1917)

Obv. yucca plant in flower with mountains in the
background, legend MEXICAN SERVICE and the dates
1911–1917; rev. trophy of arms with the legend
FOR SERVICE and UNITED STATES ARMY. Ribbon: green,
yellow and blue.

(a)   numbered   E

(b)   not numbered D

68.   NAVY MEXICAN SERVICE MEDAL (1918)

Obv. castle in Veracruz harbour with the legend
MEXICO and the dates 1911–1917; rev. as for No. 65.
Ribbon: as for No. 67.

(a)	Navy, numbered	E
(b)	Marine Corps, numbered	F
(c)	Navy, not numbered	D
(d)	Marine Corps, not numbered	E

69. <u>MEXICAN BORDER SERVICE MEDAL</u> (1918)

Obv. sheathed Roman sword over a tablet inscribed
<u>FOR SERVICE ON THE MEXICAN BORDER</u>; rev. as for No.
58. Ribbon: green and yellow.

(a)	numbered	D
(b)	not numbered	C

70. <u>PEARY POLAR EXPEDITION MEDAL</u> (1908-9)

Silver medal with obv. Admiral Peary and legend
<u>PEARY POLAR EXPEDITION</u> 1908-09 within a compass rose;
rev. US flag with eskimo dogs and the legend
<u>PRESENTED IN THE NAME OF THE CONGRESS IN RECOGNITION
OF HIS EFFORTS AND SERVICE AS A MEMBER OF THE PEARY
POLAR EXPEDITION OF 1908-09 IN THE FIELD OF SCIENCE
AND FOR THE CAUSE OF POLAR EXPEDITION BY AIDING IN
THE DISCOVERY OF THE NORTH POLE BY ADMIRAL PEARY.</u>
The name of the holder is engraved below. Ribbon:
white with blue stripes   I

71. <u>WORLD WAR I VICTORY MEDAL</u> (1919)

Obv. Winged Victory; rev. legend <u>THE GREAT WAR FOR
CIVILIZATION</u> with the US coat of arms and the names
of the Allied nations. The following clasps were
issued with this medal:
<u>CAMBRAI</u> – <u>SOMME DEFENSIVE</u> – <u>LYS</u> – <u>AISNE</u> – <u>MONTDIDIER
NOYON</u> – <u>CHAMPAGNE MARNE</u> – <u>AISNE MARNE</u> – <u>SOMME
OFFENSIVE</u> – <u>OISE AISNE</u> – <u>YPRES LYS</u> – <u>ST MIHIEL</u> –
<u>MEUSE ARGONNE</u> – <u>VITTORIO VENETO</u> – <u>DEFENSIVE SECTOR</u> –
<u>FRANCE</u> – <u>ITALY</u> – <u>SIBERIA</u> – <u>RUSSIA</u> – <u>ENGLAND</u> –
<u>OVERSEAS</u> – <u>ARMED GUARD</u> – <u>ASIATIC</u> – <u>ATLANTIC FLEET</u> –
<u>AVIATION DESTROYER</u> – <u>ESCORT</u> – <u>GRAND FLEET</u> – <u>MINE
LAYING</u> – <u>MINE SWEEPING</u> – <u>MOBILE BASE</u> – <u>NAVAL BATTERY</u> –
<u>PATROL</u> – <u>SALVAGE</u> – <u>SUB CHASER</u> – <u>SUBMARINE</u> – <u>TRANSPORT</u> –
<u>WEST INDIES</u> – <u>WHITE SEA</u>. Some of these were awarded

to the army alone, others to the navy alone and some
to both   A or B according to combination of bars

72. ARMY OF OCCUPATION OF GERMANY MEDAL (1941)

Although this medal refers to the period 1918-23 it
was not authorised until 1941. Obv. General Pershing
with the legend GENERAL JOHN J. PERSHING and the
dates 1918 and 1923; rev. eagle on Castle
Ehrenbreitstein and the legend U.S. ARMY OF OCCUPATION
OF GERMANY. Ribbon: blue, red, white and black   C

73. NAVY EXPEDITIONARY MEDAL (1936)

Awarded for a large number of small actions between
1873 and 1926. Obv. sailor beaching a boat of
marines with the legend EXPEDITIONS; rev. eagle on
naval anchor with the legend FOR SERVICE and UNITED
STATES NAVY. Ribbon: yellow and blue   C

74. MARINE CORPS EXPEDITIONARY MEDAL (1936)

Obv. a charging Marine with the legend EXPEDITIONS;
rev. as for the US Navy Medal with the legend
UNITED STATES MARINE CORPS. Ribbon: gold and scarlet.

    (a)   numbered   E

    (b)   not numbered D

75. NC-4 MEDAL (1929)

Obv. a gull in flight over waves with the legend
FIRST TRANSATLANTIC FLIGHT UNITED STATES NAVY MAY
1919; rev. legend NEWFOUNDLAND - NC-4 - PORTUGAL,
and the names of the recipients: J. H. TOWERS,
A. C. READ, E. F. STONE, W. HINTON, H. C. RODD,
J. L. BREESE, F. RHODES and PRESENTED BY THE
PRESIDENT OF THE UNITED STATES IN THE NAME OF
CONGRESS. As only seven persons received this medal
it is very rare, and there is no up-to-date
valuation, but should one come on the market its
estimated value would be   L

76.   YANGTZE SERVICE MEDAL (1930)

Obv. a Chinese junk at sea with the legend YANGTZE
SERVICE; rev. eagle on the shank of a naval anchor
and the legend FOR SERVICE. Ribbon: red, blue and
yellow.

    (a) Navy, numbered   F

    (b) Marine Corps, numbered   G

    (c) Navy, not numbered   D

    (d) Marine Corps, not numbered   D

77.   SECOND NICARAGUAN CAMPAIGN MEDAL (1929)

Obv. Columbia with sword shielding a man and a
woman; rev. as for No. 76. Ribbon: red with blue-
grey stripes.

    (a) Navy, numbered   F

    (b) Marine Corps, numbered   G

    (c) Navy, not numbered   E

    (d) Marine Corps, not numbered   F

78.   BYRD ANTARCTIC EXPEDITION MEDAL (1930)

In gold to Admiral Byrd, in silver to his officers,
and in bronze to others. Obv. Admiral Byrd in arctic
clothing with legend BYRD ANTARCTIC EXPEDITION 1928-
30; rev. sailing ship with the legend PRESENTED TO
THE OFFICERS AND MEN OF THE BYRD ANTARCTIC EXPEDITION
TO EXPRESS THE HIGH ADMIRATION IN WHICH THE CONGRESS
AND THE AMERICAN PEOPLE HOLD THEIR HEROIC AND
UNDAUNTED SERVICES IN CONNECTION WITH THE SCIENTIFIC
INVESTIGATIONS AND EXTRAORDINARY AERIAL EXPLORATION
OF THE ANTARCTIC CONTINENT. Below is a Ford trimotor
aircraft. Ribbon: white with a broad blue central
stripe.

It is not possible to give a value to the
single gold medal, the estimated value of the silver
is in the K bracket and the bronze J.

79. <u>SECOND BYRD ANTARCTIC EXPEDITION MEDAL</u> (1936)

Silver medal with obv. Admiral Byrd in arctic
clothing with an eskimo dog and the legend <u>BYRD</u>
<u>ANTARCTIC EXPEDITION</u> and the dates 1933 and 1935;
rev. a Ford trimotor aircraft, a sailing ship, a dog
team and Little America radio station, with the
legend <u>PRESENTED TO THE OFFICERS AND MEN OF THE</u>
<u>SECOND BYRD ANTARCTIC EXPEDITION TO EXPRESS THE VERY</u>
<u>HIGH ADMIRATION IN WHICH THE CONGRESS AND THE</u>
<u>AMERICAN PEOPLE HOLD THEIR HEROIC AND UNDAUNTED</u>
<u>ACCOMPLISHMENT FOR SCIENCE UNEQUALED IN THE HISTORY</u>
<u>OF POLAR EXPLORATION.</u> Ribbon: plain white   J

80. <u>CHINA SERVICE MEDAL</u> (1942)

Originally issued to cover operations in China
between July 1937 and September 1939, it was again
issued as the China Service Medal (Extended) to
cover service in China, Taiwan and Matsu Straits
during the period 1945-57. The medal remains the
same, but those entitled to it for the first period
wear a bronze star on the ribbon if they are also
entitled to it for the second period. Obv. Chinese
junk with the legend <u>CHINA SERVICE</u>; rev. as for
No. 76.

    (a) Navy   B

    (b) Marine Corps   C

81. <u>UNITED STATES ANTARCTIC EXPEDITION MEDAL</u> (1945)

Issued in gold, silver and bronze with obv. circle
with map grid lines and the legend <u>THE UNITED STATES</u>
<u>ANTARCTIC EXPEDITION</u> and the dates 1939-1941 and
<u>SOUTH PACIFIC OCEAN, LITTLE AMERICA, PALMERLAND,</u>
<u>ANTARCTICA AND SOUTH POLE</u>; rev. <u>BY ACT OF CONGRESS</u>
<u>OF THE UNITED STATES OF AMERICA TO</u> (name of recipient)
<u>IN RECOGNITION OF INVALUABLE SERVICE TO THIS NATION</u>
<u>BY COURAGEOUS PIONEERING IN POLAR EXPLORATION WHICH</u>
<u>RESULTED IN IMPORTANT GEOGRAPHICAL AND SCIENTIFIC</u>
<u>DISCOVERIES.</u> Ribbon: blue and white with narrow red
stripes. I have no recent valuation for the gold and
silver medals, but the bronze are valued   G

82. AMERICAN DEFENSE SERVICE MEDAL (1941) (Illustration No. 80)

Obv. female Grecian figure holding a sword, legend AMERICAN DEFENSE; rev. FOR SERVICE DURING THE LIMITED EMERGENCY PROCLAIMED BY THE PRESIDENT ON 8 SEPTEMBER 1939 OR DURING THE UNLIMITED EMERGENCY PROCLAIMED BY THE PRESIDENT ON 27 MAY 1941. The following clasps were issued: FOREIGN SERVICE, FLEET, BASE, SEA, bronze letter A. Ribbon: yellow with blue, white and red thin vertical stripes   B

83. AMERICAN CAMPAIGN MEDAL (1946)

Obv. aircraft, battleship and sinking submarine with some buildings, legend AMERICAN CAMPAIGN; rev. American eagle between the dates 1941-1945 and the legend UNITED STATES OF AMERICA. A bronze star has been authorised for wear on the ribbon. Ribbon: blue with white, black and red stripes   A

84. ASIATIC-PACIFIC CAMPAIGN MEDAL (1946) (Illustration No. 78)

Obv. tropical seaborne assault scene with battleship, aircraft carrier, submarine and aircraft, legend ASIATIC-PACIFIC CAMPAIGN; rev. as for No. 83. Ribbon: yellow with white, red and black thin vertical stripes   A

85. EUROPEAN-AFRICAN-MIDDLE EASTERN CAMPAIGN MEDAL (1946) (Illustration No. 81)

Obv. landing craft and troops landing with the legend EUROPEAN-AFRICAN-MIDDLE EASTERN CAMPAIGN; rev. as for No. 83. Ribbon: brown, green, white, red, black and blue vertical stripes   A

86. WOMEN'S ARMY CORPS SERVICE MEDAL (1943)

Obv. head of Pallas Athene over a sheathed sword with the legend WOMEN'S ARMY CORPS; rev. thirteen stars and a scroll with the legend FOR SERVICE IN THE WOMEN'S ARMY AUXILIARY CORPS, an eagle and the

dates 1942–1943. Ribbon: green with two yellow
stripes on the edges   B

87.   WORLD WAR II VICTORY MEDAL (1945)

Obv. figure of Liberation with the legend WORLD WAR
II; rev. UNITED STATES OF AMERICA 1941–1945 in a
circle and within this FREEDOM FROM FEAR AND WANT
FREEDOM OF SPEECH AND RELIGION. Ribbon: double
rainbow with a broad red stripe in the centre   A

88.   MERCHANT MARINE VICTORY MEDAL (1946)

Obv. allegorical figure holding a trident and the
legend WORLD WAR II. Ribbon: vertical stripes of red,
white, blue, brown and yellow   D

89.   ARMY OF OCCUPATION MEDAL (1949)

Obv. Remagen Bridge and the legend ARMY OF OCCUPATION;
rev. Mount Fuji, two Japanese sailing vessels and
the date 1946. The Berlin Airlift device is authorised
for wear on this ribbon. Ribbon: white, black, red
and white   B

90.   NAVY OCCUPATION SERVICE MEDAL (1947)

Obv. Neptune on a sea serpent and waves, legend
OCCUPATION SERVICE; rev. as for No. 66 The Berlin
Airlift device is authorised for wear on this ribbon.
Ribbon: as above.

      (a) Navy   B

      (b) Marine Corps rev.   C

91.   MEDAL FOR HUMANE ACTION (1949)

Obv. C–54 aircraft within a wreath of wheat with the
coat of arms of Berlin underneath; rev. American
eagle with the legend FOR HUMANE ACTION and TO SUPPLY
NECESSITIES OF LIFE TO THE PEOPLE OF BERLIN, GERMANY.
Ribbon: vertical stripes of black, white, blue and
red   B

92. <u>NATIONAL DEFENSE SERVICE MEDAL</u> (1953) (Illustration
     No. 77)

     Obv. eagle with the legend <u>NATIONAL DEFENSE</u>; rev.
     shield and wreath. Ribbon: <u>vertical stripes</u> in broad
     red, narrow white, blue and red, with wide central
     yellow one   A

93. <u>KOREAN SERVICE MEDAL</u> (1950)

     Obv. Korean gateway with the legend <u>KOREAN SERVICE</u>;
     rev. Korean symbol taken from the <u>centre of the</u>
     Korean national flag and the legend <u>UNITED STATES OF
     AMERICA</u>. Ribbon: blue with two white <u>stripes</u>   B

94. <u>ANTARCTICA SERVICE MEDAL</u> (1960)

     Green-gold colour of metal with obv. man in arctic
     clothing between the words <u>ANTARCTICA</u> and <u>SERVICE</u>;
     rev. <u>COURAGE</u>, <u>SACRIFICE</u> and <u>DEVOTION</u>, superimposed
     on <u>polar projection</u>. Ribbon: black, blue and white
     on which a <u>WINTERED-OVER</u> clasp in bronze, silver or
     gold is <u>worn, for one or</u> more winters' service   D

95. <u>ARMED FORCES EXPEDITIONARY MEDAL</u> (1962)

     Awarded to cover operations from 1958 onwards for
     which no special medals have been issued. Obv. eagle
     over a compass rose with the legend <u>ARMED FORCES</u> and
     <u>EXPEDITIONARY SERVICE</u>; rev. coat of <u>arms of the</u> USA
     <u>with the legend UNITED</u> STATES OF AMERICA. Ribbon:
     vertical green, <u>yellow, brown, black, light</u> and dark
     blue, white and red stripes   A

96. <u>VIETNAM SERVICE MEDAL</u> (1965)

     Obv. dragon behind bamboo trees with the legend
     <u>REPUBLIC OF VIETNAM SERVICE</u>; rev. crossbow with a
     <u>torch above and the legend</u> UNITED STATES OF AMERICA.
     Ribbon: yellow with thin green and red vertical
     stripes   A

RUSSIA

1. <u>ORDER OF ST ANDREW</u> (1698)

The senior Russian order which had one class only.
The badge consists of a double-headed black and gold
eagle, with spread wings, upon which a blue saltire
of St Andrew with effigy of the saint. Letters
S.A.P.R. on the badge. The badge is suspended by a
gold and red enamel imperial crown from a collar, or
from a blue sash on less formal occasions. The star
had the eagle and cross surrounded by the motto in
the centre. Very rare no valuation.

2. <u>ORDER OF THE WHITE EAGLE</u> (1705)

Originated in Poland, and became a Russian order in
1831. One class only. Badge similar to No. 1 above,
with black double-headed eagle with outstretched
wings with a white enamel eagle superimposed on a
cross with V-shaped ends, in red enamel with white
edges, resting upon a star with golden rays. The
badge hangs from an imperial crown from a dark-blue
sash, and a star is worn on the left breast.
Valuation varies according to the period and the
richness of the insignia, but usually J - K

3. <u>ORDER OF ST ALEXANDER NEVSKY</u> (1725)

One class. The badge consists of a red enamel cross,
with gold edges, and double-headed gold eagles
between the arms of the cross. A circular badge in
the centre of the cross shows the saint on horseback.
The badge hangs from a scarlet sash and a breast
star is worn at the same time.

        (a) badge and star   L

        (b) star alone   I

4.   <u>ORDER OF ST ANNE</u> (1735)

Originally a civilian order, it became a military one
as well, when, after 1855, it was awarded with swords.
Gold cross pattée in dark-red enamel with gold edges,
gold design between the arms of the cross and St
Anne in the centre of the cross. Crossed swords
between the arms of the cross.

    (a) 1st Cl., Knight Commander, sash badge J
                                      breast star G

    (b) 2nd Cl., Commander, gold and enamel
        neck badge H

    (c) 3rd Cl., Companion, neck badge H

    (d) Medal of the Order E

5.   <u>ORDER OF ST STANISLAS</u> (1765)

Gold Maltese cross enamelled in dark red, with small
gold balls at each point of the cross, the white
Polish eagle in gold between the arms of the cross,
in the centre the letters <u>SS</u> entwined over a white-
enamel background surroun<u>de</u>d by a wreath. Awarded
with crossed swords for war service, the swords
being between the arms of the cross.

    (a) 1st Cl., Knight Grand Cross, gold and
        enamel badge and breast star I

    (b) 2nd Cl., Commander, neck badge, in gold
        and enamel G

    (c) 3rd Cl., Companion, breast badge F

6.   <u>ORDER OF ST GEORGE</u> (1769)

White enamelled gold cross pattée with St George and
the dragon in a circle at the centre of the cross on
the obv., and the saint's initials on the rev.
The star is a gold diamond-shaped plaque with initials
in the centre and a circle round the legend <u>FOR
SERVICE AND FOR BRAVERY</u> in Russian, in gold letters.
Ribbon: orange with three black stripes.

    (a) 1st Cl., as described above J

(b) 2nd Cl., neck badge, smaller in diameter,
        and breast star   I

(c) 3rd Cl., neck badge   F

(d) 4th Cl., breast badge   C

Various medals connected with this order have been
issued in gold, silver and bronze. Their prices vary
a great deal: silver medals are in brackets C-D,
bronze and white-metal ones in brackets B-C. I have
no recent valuation for the gold.

7.   <u>ORDER OF ST VLADIMIR</u> (1782)

Became a military order in the 1850s when awarded
with swords. Cross pattée in gold, enamelled dark
red with black edges and a thin fillet of gold round
the black enamel. On a circular black-enamel disc
with, in the centre, the imperial mantle with the
imperial cipher surmounted by a crown. The swords
are between the arms of the cross.

(a) 1st Cl., Knight Grand Cross, sash badge I
                                 breast star H

(b) 2nd Cl., Knight Commander, gold and
        enamel neck badge   H

(c) 3rd Cl., Commander, gold and enamel
        breast badge   F

(d) 4th Cl., Companion, gold and enamel
        breast badge   E

(e) Medal of the Order   D

8.   <u>MEDALS FOR ZEAL IN WAR</u>

Obv. eagle with Serbian arms; rev. Russian
inscription <u>FOR DEVOTED SERVICE</u> within a laurel
wreath. Ribbon: dark blue, which became red during
WW I.

(a) gold   H

(b) silver   D

(c) white metal (later issue) C

9. <u>MEDALS FOR BRAVERY</u>

Obv. effigy of Obilitch in armour on the obv. with
the names in Serbian letters Miloch Obilitch; rev.
cross pattée with swords and, within a wreath, the
legend <u>FOR BRAVERY</u>. Ribbon: red.

> (a) gold   H
> (b) silver C

10. <u>HUNGARIAN UPRISING MEDAL</u> (1849)

Silver   C

11. <u>CRIMEAN WAR MEDAL 1854-6</u>

Bronze   C

12. <u>DEFENCE OF SEBASTOPOOL MEDAL 1856</u>

Silver   D

13. <u>TURKISH WAR MEDAL 1877-8</u>

> (a) silver   D
> (b) bronze   C

14. <u>RUSSO JAPANESE WAR MEDAL 1904-5</u>

Bronze   C

15. <u>MEDAL COMMEMORATIVE OF THE 1812 WAR</u> (1912)

Gilt bronze   C

16. <u>ROMANOV TERCENTENARY MEDAL 1613-1913</u>

Gilt bronze   B

17. <u>ALEXANDER III COMMEMORATIVE MEDAL 1881-94</u>

Bronze   C

USSR

1. <u>GOLD STAR MEDAL</u>

   Five-pointed gold star worn above all other
   decorations and hanging from a red ribbon   G

2. <u>ORDER OF VICTORY</u> (1943)

   Badge made of platinum with five-pointed ruby star,
   bordered with diamonds. Rays between the points of
   the star also studded with diamonds. In the centre
   of the emblem, Kremlin Wall and Spassky Tower
   surrounded by a laurel and oak wreath. Ribbon: red
   with narrow green, dark-blue, red, light-blue and
   white stripes. Edging of orange, black and orange
   narrow stripes. Very rare no valuation

3. <u>MARSHAL'S STAR</u>

   Five-pointed gold star with smaller diamond-studded
   star in the centre. There is also a diamond between
   each ray of the star. Worn round the neck from a red
   ribbon for marshals of the Soviet Union, gold for
   artillery marshals, pale blue for air marshals, and
   deep red for tank and mechanised-unit marshals.
   Also very rare no valuation

4. <u>ORDER OF THE RED BANNER</u> (1932)

   Laurel wreath over the upper part of which is the
   Red Flag with the legend <u>WORKERS OF ALL COUNTRIES
   UNITE</u>, behind a hammer and a plough, in the centre
   a red star with the hammer and sickle. USSR in
   Russian on a red enamel riband at the bottom F

   with 2 superimposed for second award   G

5.   <u>ORDER OF SUVOROV</u> (1942)

Five-pointed star with radiating beams with the head
of Marshal Suvorov in the centre with the legend
<u>ALEXANDER SUVOROV</u> in Russian. Normally worn without
ribbon.

     (a)   1st Cl., in platinum with the centre in
         matt gold, and awarded to high-ranking
         officers of the three services   no recent
         valuation

     (b)   2nd Cl., issued to corps, divisional and
         brigade commanders, in silver and silver
         gilt   no recent valuation

     (c)   3rd Cl., all silver; awarded to regimental
         and battalion commanders   G

6.   <u>ORDER OF KUTUZOV</u>

Badge in the shape of a star, five-pointed with
radiating beams. White-enamel centre with the head
of Marshal Kutuzov with the Kremlin Tower in the
background and the name Michael Kutuzov. Silver rays
between the points of the star. The insignia are
worn without ribbon. There are three classes:

     (a)   1st Cl., issued to commanders of fronts
         and armies, gold and silver badge
         no recent valuation

     (b)   2nd Cl., issued to corps, divisional and
         brigade commanders, in silver and silver
         gilt   no recent valuation

     (c)   3rd Cl., issued to regimental and battalion
         commanders, completely in silver   G

7.   <u>ORDER OF ALEXANDER NEVSKY</u> (1942)

One class only. Red-enamel, five-pointed star on a
ten-pointed silver background. In the centre the
effigy of Prince and General Alexander Nevsky with
battle-axes above. Hammer and sickle below the effigy.
Ribbon: pale blue with central red stripe   F

214

8. <u>ORDER OF GLORY</u> (1943)

Five-pointed star with the Kremlin and the Spassky
Tower, two sprays of laurels and <u>GLORY</u> in Russian in
the centre. Ribbon: orange with <u>three</u> black stripes.
There are three classes: 1st Cl., gold, 2nd Cl.,
silver with gold centre, 3rd Cl., silver   all E

9. <u>ORDER OF THE PATRIOTIC WAR</u>

Red star with hammer and sickle in the centre,
behind which are a sword and a rifle surrounded by
sunrays and the legend round the centre <u>PATRIOTIC WAR</u>
in Russian on a white background.

    (a) 1st Cl., gold   G
    (b) 2nd Cl., silver   F

10. <u>ORDER OF USHAKOV</u>

Naval award, in the shape of a five-pointed star on
which a large silver anchor is superimposed, on which,
within circles of ropes and chains, is the effigy of
Admiral Ushakov in naval uniform. Worn without ribbon.

    (a) 1st Cl., with centre medallion in gold   F
    (b) 2nd Cl., with centre medallion in silver   E

There is also a medal to this order which consists
of the centre medallion and anchor, hanging from a
V-shaped chain. Ribbon: pale blue with dark blue and
white stripes   C

11. <u>ORDER OF NAKIMOV</u>

Also a naval award. Badge in the shape of a five-
pointed star between the points of which are anchors,
crowns and flukes. The centre has the effigy of
Admiral Nakimov.

    (a) 1st Cl., gold   F
    (b) 2nd Cl., silver   E

The medal of the order is gold and has the same

design as described above. It has a pale-blue ribbon
with three white stripes   F

12. <u>ORDER OF BOGDAN KHMELNITSKY</u>

The badge is made up of a ten-pointed star with a
portrait of Bogdan Khmelnitsky in the centre. The
1st Cl. insignia has five gold rays and five silver
ones, whilst the 2nd and 3rd Cl. have ten silver
rays. Ribbon: pale blue and white with a centre
stripe for the 1st Cl., white edges for the 2nd Cl.,
and both for the 3rd Cl.   all D

13. <u>ORDER OF THE RED STAR</u> (1930)

Red-star badge with, in the centre, a Russian
soldier holding a rifle, above the legend <u>WORKERS OF
ALL COUNTRIES, UNITE</u> and below USSR, both in
Russian. One class only, worn without a ribbon   D

14. <u>MEDAL FOR VALOUR</u> (1938)

Silver medal enamelled red and white with a tank and
aeroplane and the legend <u>FOR VALOUR</u> and <u>USSR</u>. Ribbon:
pale grey with blue stripes at the edges   C

15. <u>MEDAL FOR DISTINGUISHED SERVICE</u>

Similar design to the previous one, but with crossed
rifle and sword and the legend <u>FOR DISTINGUISHED
BATTLE SERVICE - USSR</u>. Ribbon: same, but with yellow
edging   C

16. <u>RED ARMY LONG SERVICE MEDALS</u> (1938)

Silver medal with red enamelled five-pointed star
with gold edging.

        (a) for twenty years' service, Roman numerals
             <u>XX</u> on the medal, and grey ribbon with
             narrow red edges   C

        (b) for thirty years' service, as above but
             <u>XXX</u>, and the ribbon is grey with red
             central stripe and red edges   D

216

17. <u>PARTISAN MEDAL</u>

Obv. effigies of Lenin and Stalin with the legend
<u>TO A PARTISAN OF THE PATRIOTIC WAR</u>.

  (a) silver, with bright-green ribbon with
     narrow red centre stripe C

  (b) bronze, do., but the stripe is blue
     instead of red   B

18. <u>MEDAL FOR THE VICTORY OVER GERMANY</u> (1945)

Obv. Stalin in uniform facing left; rev. plain.
Mottoes <u>OUR CAUSE IS JUST</u> and <u>WE ARE VICTORIOUS</u>.
Ribbon: orange with three black stripes. Bronze B

19. <u>MEDAL FOR THE VICTORY OVER JAPAN</u> (1945)

As above, but Stalin faces right, and the ribbon has
yellow edges; rev. plain C

20. <u>MEDAL FOR THE 800TH ANNIVERSARY OF MOSCOW</u> (1947)

Bronze B

21. <u>LIBERATION OF WARSAW MEDAL</u> (1945)

Sun-burst with a star and the legend <u>WARSAW</u> and <u>FOR</u>
<u>THE LIBERATION OF WARSAW</u>; rev. plain. Bronze.
Ribbon: blue, red, blue with yellow edges C

22. <u>LIBERATION OF BELGRADE</u> (1945)

Obv. <u>FOR THE LIBERATION OF BELGRADE</u> within a wreath;
rev. plain. Bronze. Ribbon: green, black, green C

23. <u>LIBERATION OF PRAGUE</u> (1945)

Sun-burst and wreath with the legend <u>FOR THE</u>
<u>LIBERATION OF PRAGUE</u> on the obv., rev. plain.
Bronze. Ribbon: mauve, blue, mauve C

24. <u>CAPTURE OF BERLIN MEDAL</u> (1945)

Bronze medal with an obv. oak leaves and a star with

the legend FOR THE CAPTURE OF BERLIN; rev. plain.
Ribbon: red, black and orange   C

25.   CAPTURE OF VIENNA MEDAL (1945)

Bronze medal with on obv. a star, a wreath and the
legend FOR THE CAPTURE OF VIENNA; rev. plain. Ribbon:
pale blue, dark blue and pale blue   C

26.   CAPTURE OF BUDAPEST MEDAL (1945)

Bronze medal with a star, the hammer and sickle
surrounded by two branches and in the centre FOR THE
CAPTURE OF BUDAPEST; rev. plain. Ribbon: orange, pale
blue and orange   C

27.   CAPTURE OF KOENIGSBERG MEDAL (1945)

Bronze medal, with a radiant star and a branch, and
the legend FOR THE CAPTURE OF KOENIGSBERG; rev. plain.
Ribbon: green with three black stripes   C

28.   DEFENCE OF THE CAUCASUS MEDAL

Obv. mountain with aeroplanes, oil wells and tanks,
legend FOR THE DEFENCE OF THE CAUCASUS; rev. plain.
Ribbon: olive-green with blue edges, and narrow blue,
white, green, red, white and blue stripes   C

29.   DEFENCE OF THE SOVIET ARCTIC MEDAL (1944)

Bronze medal with a soldier in arctic clothing with
a tank, a warship and an aeroplane. Legend FOR THE
DEFENCE OF SOVIET ARCTIC. Ribbon: pale blue, pale
green and pale blue, with narrow white stripes and
edges   D

30.   DEFENCE OF LENINGRAD MEDAL (1942)

Bronze medal with on obv. three soldiers in front of
a tower and around the legend FOR THE DEFENCE OF
LENINGRAD; rev. plain. Ribbon: olive-green with
narrow dark green central stripe   C

31. <u>DEFENCE OF STALINGRAD MEDAL</u>

Bronze with obv. five soldiers in front of a red
flag. Legend <u>FOR THE DEFENCE OF STALINGRAD</u>; rev.
plain. Ribbon: olive-green with narrow red central
stripe   C

32. <u>DEFENCE OF MOSCOW MEDAL</u>

Bronze with a tank and the Kremlin, a wreath underneath, and the legend <u>FOR THE DEFENCE OF MOSCOW</u>; rev.
plain. Ribbon: red with three olive stripes   C

33. <u>DEFENCE OF ODESSA MEDAL</u>

Bronze with obv. a soldier and a sailor advancing,
below a wreath, above the legend <u>FOR THE DEFENCE OF
ODESSA</u>; rev. plain. Ribbon: olive-green with pale
blue central stripe   C

34. <u>30TH JUBILEE OF THE SOVIET ARMY AND NAVY MEDAL</u> (1948)

Bronze   C

35. <u>40TH ANNIVERSARY OF THE SOVIETY ARMY MEDAL 1918-58</u>

C

36. <u>50TH JUBILEE OF THE SOVIET ARMED FORCES MEDAL 1918-
68</u>

C

37. <u>20TH ANNIVERSARY OF WORLD WAR II MEDAL 1945-65</u>

Bronze   B

38. <u>250TH ANNIVERSARY OF THE FOUNDING OF LENINGRAD 1957</u>

Bronze   B

39. <u>GOOD CONDUCT MEDAL</u> (1958)

1st Cl., silver and red enamel, 2nd Cl., enamel,
3rd Cl., bronze   all B

SELECT BIBLIOGRAPHY

GENERAL

BRESSON, JACQUES. Précis historique des ordres de chevalerie, décorations militaires et civiles reconnues et conférées actuellement par les souverains régnants en Europe et dans les états des autres parties du monde. Paris, 1844

BURKE, SIR BERNARD. The Book of Orders of Knighthood and Decorations of Honour. London, 1858

DORLING, CAPT H. TAPPRELL. Ribbons and Medals. Revised L. F. Guille, London, 1916; numerous revised and enlarged editions since

JOHNSON, S. C. The Medal Collector. London, 1921

PAYNE, DR A. A. A Handbook of British and Foreign Orders, War Medals and Decorations. Sheffield, 1911

PURVES, ALEC A. Collecting Medals and Decorations. London, 1968

___. Orders and Decorations. London, 1972

SANDWICH, EARL OF. British and Foreign Medals Relating to Naval and Maritime Affairs. London, 1950

STEWARD, W. A. War Medals and Their History. London, 1915

WERLICH, ROBERT. Orders and Decorations of All Nations. London, 1965

AUSTRALIA

DOWNEY, M. The Standard Catalogue of Orders, Decorations

and Medals Awarded to Australians, with Valuations. Sydney, 1971

AUSTRIA

FALKENSTEIN, JOSEPH VON. Imperial Austrian Medals and Decorations. Hyrum, Utah 1972

MICHETSCHLAGER, H. Das Ordensbuch des Gewesenen Osterreichisch-Ungarischen Monarchie. Vienna, 1919

ROSENFELD,F. H. VON. Die Orden und Ehrenzeichen des K und K Osterreichisch-Ungarischen Monarchies. Vienna, 1899

BELGIUM

GUIOTH, . Histoire numismatique de la révolution belge. Brussels, 1844

HOLLEBEKE, VAN. Histoire et législation des ordres de chevalerie et marques d'honneur du royaume de Belgique. Brussels, 1879

QUINOT, H. Recueil illustré des ordres de chevalerie et décorations belges de 1830 à 1963. Brussels, 1964

CANADA

IRWIN, ROSS W. War Medals and Decorations of Canada. Guelph, Ont, 1969

DENMARK

JØRGENSEN, CAPT P. J. Danish Orders and Medals. Copenhagen, 1964

FRANCE

D'AMANDE, A. Légion d'honneur, médailles militaires ou commémoratives, ordres étrangers. Paris, 1873

ANCHEL, R. et CAILLE, P. F. Histoire des décorations francaise contemporaines. Paris, 1933

BONNEVILLE DE MARSANGY. La Légion d'honneur. Paris, 1900

BOURDIER,   . Les Ordres francais et les récompenses
    nationales. Paris, 1926

BUCQUET, DURIEUX et FEUILLATRE. La Légion d'honneur et les
    décorations francaises. Paris, 1911

COLLEVILLE ET SAINT-CHRISTO, COMTE DE. Les Ordres du roi
    de 1099 à 1830. Paris, 1830

DELANDE, M. Les décorations de France et de ses colonies.
    Paris, 1934

DELARBRE, J. La Légion d'honneur. Paris, 1887

RENAULT, JULES. La médaille militaire. Paris, 1934

___. La Légion d'honneur et les anciens ordres francais
    de chevalerie. Paris, 1932

STEENACKER,   . Histoire des ordres de chevalerie et des
    distinctions honorifiques en France. Paris, 1867

___. Décorations officielles francaises. Issued by
    l'Administration des Monnaies et Medailles. Paris, 1956;
    with supplement 1967

GERMANY

DOEHLE, DR H. Orden und Ehrenzeichen in Gross-Deutschland.
    Berlin, 1941

HESSENTHAL & SCHREIBER. Die Tragbare Ehrenzeichen des
    Deutschen Reiches. Berlin, 1940

KLIETMANN, DR K. G. Für Tapferkeit und Verdienst. Munich,
    1955

PROWSE, A. E. The Iron Cross of Prussia and Germany.
    Upper Hutt, NZ, 1971

GREAT BRITAIN

CARTER, T. Medals of the British Army and How They Were
    Won. London, 1861

COLE, LT-COL H. N. _Coronation and Commemorative Medals 1887-1953_. Aldershot, 1953

GORDON, MAJOR L. L. _British Battles and Medals_. Aldershot, 1947; and later editions

___. _British Orders and Awards_. London, 1968

HANSON, I. M. _A Simplified Catalogue of British Campaign Medals, Awards and Decorations_, Vol 1. Newcastle-upon-Tyne, 1970

IRWIN, D. HASTINGS. _War Medals and Decorations_. London, 1890; and later editions

JOSLIN, E. C. _The Standard Catalogue of British Orders, Decorations and Medals_. London, 3rd ed 1976

LONG, W. H. _Medals of the British Navy_. London, 1895

MAYO, J. H. _Medals and Decorations of the British Army and Navy_. London, 1897

POULSON, MAJOR N. W. _The White Ribbon: A Medallic Record of British Polar Expeditions_. London, 1968

___. _A Catalogue of Campaign and Independence Medals Issued During the Twentieth Century to the British Army_. Newcastle-upon-Tyne, 1969

WILSON, SIR ARNOLD and MCEWEN, CAPT J. H. F. _Gallantry_. London, 1939

___. _Statutes of the Most Excellent Order of the British Empire_. London, 1954

INDIA

State Decorations and Awards (Government of India publication). Delhi, 1958

IRELAND

O'TOOLE, WING-COMMANDER E. H. _Decorations and Medals of the Republic of Ireland_. London, 1972

ITALY

CESCHINA, R. E. <u>Gli ordini equestri del regno d'Italia</u>.
   Rome, 1938

MORINI, UGO. <u>Gli ordini cavallereschi</u>. Rome, 1932

LUXEMBOURG

SCHLEIGH DE BOSSE, J. R. <u>Distinctions honorifiques au pays
   de Luxembourg 1430-1961</u>. Luxembourg, 1962

NETHERLANDS

BAX, DR W. F. <u>De Nederlandse Ridderorden en
   Onderscheidingen</u>. Rotterdam, 1951

PORTUGAL

<u>Forces armées Portuguaises</u> (Portuguese Government
   publication). Lisbon, 1960

RUSSIA

HURLEY, C. <u>Russian Orders, Decorations and Medals</u>.
   London, 1934

SPAIN

PUENTE Y GOMEZ, F. F. DE LA. <u>Conderaciones Espanolas</u>.
   Madrid, 1953

USA

GIBBONS, C. <u>Military Decorations and Campaign Bars of
   U.S.A.</u> (issued privately). Wilton, Conn, 1945

ROBLES, P. K. <u>United States Military Medals and Ribbons</u>.
   Rutland, Vt, 1971